HANDBAGS AND POOBAGS

TALES OF A SOHO BOXER DOG

ALICE WRIGHT

**‘*Handbags and Poobags:*
Tales of a Soho Boxer Dog’**

First published in 2012 by Alice Wright

Line from "*Do not go gentle into that good night*"
by Dylan Thomas,
originally published in 1951, Botteghe Oscure

Original artwork by Patrick O'Donnell
www.patrick-odonnell.co.uk

Cover artwork by Julia Claxton
http://photography.juliaclaxton.net

PRAISE FOR *HANDBAGS AND POOBAGS: TALES OF A SOHO BOXER DOG*

"I think Alice Wright is really Bridget Bones!
Handbags and Poobags…. and bags of laughs too.
A love story with a twist in its very waggy tail.
If you're contemplating settling down with a good dog, read
this first and if it doesn't put you off then you'll be fine.
Already had your heart stolen by a dog? You'll definitely
recognise the dogification of your wardrobe, the permanent
damage to your flooring and especially the gritty bed linen!
What a page-turner. I Loved it."
Beverley Cuddy, Editor DOGS TODAY MAGAZINE

"Heartwarming and hilarious,
a must for all dog owners.
A lovely story"
Becky Sherriff, THE KINDLE BOOK REVIEW

"Incredibly honest, genuine and captivating…
A real life take on modern day doggie living.
It's brutally honest yet heart-warmingly brilliant.
A must for all animal fans"
Jessica Brown, PETS MAGAZINE

TWO THINGS YOU NEED TO KNOW

BEFORE READING THIS BOOK:

1. This is not a dog training manual

2. The dog does not die at the end

If dog-trainer Donald McCaig is to be believed

if you live with a dog you

'share the thoughts, habits, tics and aspirations

of a genuinely alien mind'...

so then why would you expect anything to go as

planned?

PROLOGUE: THE CONTENTS OF A HANDBAG

Soho, 3am.

I'm standing on the side of the road, neon signs flickering all around me, I'm scanning the traffic for the yellow light of an available taxi-cab. I clutch my expensive handbag to my chest as I sway drunkenly from side to side and rub my blurry eyes. I've had a great night out, dining in a beautiful restaurant and drinking in a private members bar with my girlfriends. But now I need to get home. Realising that my chances of flagging down a cab are vastly reduced by displays of drunken behaviour I straighten up and rifle through my bag for a hairbrush.

Current contents of my handbag:
- A crushed packet of cigarettes (Silk Cut)
- Two cigarette lighters (borrowed, never given back)
- Purse, keys, mobile phone (obviously)

- Lipstick (dubious origin, not my colour)
- Spare underwear (just in case)
- A small but heavy ashtray in the shape of a letter (stolen from said restaurant)
- Broken pens (ink everywhere)
- Some business cards, a bit soaked in booze (one of them has a phone number written on it)
- No hairbrush (I think I must have left it in the

  toilets of the bar?) Bugger!

Still, it could be worse. I could have found a puddle of cold vomit.

Yes, I've been sick in my own handbag before. I was incredibly hungover one morning and it was all I had with me that was suitable. I was in a taxi with my (also very hungover) flatmate on our way to work and we were both late, we'd been to a magazine party the night before and were now feeling the awful after effects of our fun evening out. I knew if I was sick in the car we would be unceremoniously dumped by the side of the road, so there was nothing for it - I opened up my bag and let it go.

My friend immediately clocked what was going on and asked the cab-driver to turn the radio up because she *'loved this song'* and proceeded to sing along loudly as I retched. (We had to give up using that cab firm eventually as both of us pretended to be pregnant so many times in order to explain having to pull in by the side of the road so we could throw up it was starting to get suspicious that neither of us were growing any bigger!) I made the mistake of admitting the handbag incident to someone at work and suddenly I became known as the *'girl who was sick in her handbag'* in the office.

This was before I was known as the *'girl who was sick in her hat'*. Yes, that happened too. One morning on the bus going down Oxford Street after a particularly big night out in the latest new bar to open up in Soho I felt the familiar nausea, I anxiously looked around me for a suitable receptacle as I tried to keep swallowing the liquid that was fast filling my mouth. As I stood up to rush off the bus and hopefully find a roadside bin events sadly overtook me, I was going to be sick right there and then. I yanked the hat (new, grey woollen beret, expensive) off my head and threw up into it, much to the horror of every other passenger. Mustering as much dignity as I could, I stepped off the bus holding the dripping hat out in front of me and walked to office with it. I was loathe to throw it away because it was new and I really liked it. Surely I could wash it out later that night?

On arrival at work I sealed it into a carrier and popped it under my desk. Later that day a colleague walked into my office and remarked: *'It smells like sick babies in here'*. Only if they had been drinking vodka! I confessed to my crime, causing much office hilarity. I believe it even went round on a 'Copy All Office' email.

Or there was the time I found some cold chips in my handbag one morning. I don't remember how they got there, but on the way home from some awards ceremony we'd been to the night before we must have thought food was a good idea and bought them.

I do remember waking up in bed to the sound of my mobile phone ringing:

"*Where are you?*" It was my boss.

"*I'm in bed*"

I'd slept through my alarm, or forgotten to set it.

"*You're meant to be here. Right now*"

Ah yes, that important client meeting that was taking place at 9am.

"*I'm on my way*".

Stepping out of bed into some clothes on the floor, I picked up my bag and stepped out of the flat without pausing to brush my hair or teeth, I stepped onto a bus that seemed to be just outside my house and 20 minutes later stepped into the meeting, all apologies. I sat down and opened my handbag to get some chewing gum (last night's furry tongue was now a harsh reality) only to reveal a cold, congealed bag of uneaten chips. Funny how old chips can still smell just like chips the morning after. Maybe it's the vinegar? Everyone looked at me in disgust. Well, at least it wasn't a kebab?

But that was all a long time ago... a long, long time ago. My days of hangover-induced throwing up, staying out late and carrying expensive handbags with rather disconcerting contents are long gone. These days I am far more likely to be found with a carrier bag full of supermarket shopping, or a doggy poobag. The little black plastic sacks carried by dog owners everywhere. The contents of which probably don't need describing...

Chapter 1: THE AGE OF INNOCENCE

I always assumed I was one of those people who loved animals. But I knew I loved my responsibility free life more. When discussing pets I would always confidently nod my head and agree that *'yes I would love a dog'* or *'your cat is so cute'*, without really thinking about it and congratulating myself on living what could be termed as a rather hedonistic existence.

Despite having lived with a couple of dogs as a youngster – owned by my mother's boyfriends and nothing to do with me (I largely ignored them or saw them as a nuisance that had to be walked when I would rather be listening to records in my room) – I had no real experience of owning my own dog and was largely indifferent to their existence.

My track record with other pets wasn't good! I'd had three hamsters as a young girl, all called Bam-Bam (only distinguished by numbers 1, 2 and 3). I tried to make them into mini-ponies and made my dolls ride them around makeshift racecourses. And all had met their end in a rather odd fashion.... 1 was found sat on and squashed under a sofa cushion, 2 starved because I'd fed it nothing but my toast crumbs for weeks because I didn't know where to buy food for it and 3 went up the Hoover. To this day I believe youngsters shouldn't keep pets without constant supervision, and I still feel bad about the Bam-Bams (especially 3).

But because I considered myself an 'animal lover' I always thought it would be in my future to have one and often discussed the merits of owning a chinchilla over having a human boyfriend with my mates.

Chinchillas are suited to the single girl's lifestyle because they are:

- nocturnal by nature (great for when you come home late and want to play)
- clean and virtually odourless
- hilarious to watch
- very soft and cuddly

But my life was already packed. I was (and still am) the company director of a small but successful entertainment public relations agency and with an office based in the heart of Soho I didn't lack opportunities for fun. My world consisted of parties, premieres and private members clubs, lacked responsibility or liability, and I loved it.

I have always relished freedom and my social life. How does one carry on such an existence when you have small furry mouths to feed at home? There was no room for accountability when you like being able to say yes to any invitation or go to one of the many Soho nightspots at the drop of a hat (hopefully a vomit free one).

Still I flirted with the idea of animal ownership just so everyone would still consider me that animal lover, and had a few hilarious discussions with my flatmate when we shared a beautiful maisonette in Notting Hill. We decided that a kitten would be a good idea and made plenty of plans for our new little charge as we sat chatting late into the night over bottles of wine. We even came up with a name for her.

But we knew that the probable fate of 'Kitty Petal' would be to end up impaled by a stiletto heel onto our spiral staircase (the result of one of us staggering drunkenly upstairs and oblivious to a small furry scrap of cat asleep on the step). No it was probably not a good idea. And besides we never had anything to eat in the house, only wine and takeaway menus, we'd certainly never remember to buy cat food. Or could kittens eat Broccoli in Oyster Sauce? We weren't sure.

A visiting friend asked us to consider getting a really, really big dog. Over a booze-fuelled debate he tried to convince us that massive hounds such as Great Danes didn't really need a lot of walking or attention and could probably sleep under said spiral staircase for about 20 hours a day, only raising their colossal heads to acknowledge our coming home after work. He actually curled up into the spot to illustrate a suitable sleeping arrangement and insisted it was the perfect city dog. But I wasn't really sure, it would be like having Jabba The Hut waiting for you at home, and my flatmate did look a little bit like Princess Leia.

(This is the flatmate who managed to drunkenly fall down a full flight of stairs in a rather well-to-do restaurant on one memorable night out – right from the top to the bottom – landing in a crumpled heap at the feet of the maître d' who, with hands on his hips asked in a rather arch manner: *'Shall I call Madame a cab? Or an ambulance?'* Ah we used to have such fun together).

Besides, I was single, successful, carefree, happy. I had designer dresses hanging in my wardrobe and plenty of men to date. What could possibly be missing? Well it turns out that before I got the dog, I got the boyfriend! I'd managed to bypass even getting a chinchilla.

I really didn't want a boyfriend when I met Patrick, I had recently finished a rather boring relationship and my beloved Granddad had just died, emotionally I was all over the place. So I told him I was only after sex and fun, and I wasn't short of either thank you very much.

Patrick and I were old friends. Well not really, he was my client and for anyone else who works in an agency you'll understand how shocking this would be for everyone else? It's not really the done thing. We dated secretly for a while which led to quite a few cat and mouse chases around town as we attempted to meet up behind the back of the party crowd. Oh and plenty of private looks in important meetings that I can still giggle and blush about to this day.

I told him of my chinchilla musings and the first present he ever bought me was a book on their upkeep. He was a big animal lover and had recently come out of a dog-owning relationship. Over our late night romancing he told me of the possibility of keeping one. Could it be true? Could people like me keep animals for real? Without them dying? I wanted to test the theory out, so for one of our very first dates that didn't involve going to a bar, we decided to spend the day at Discover Dogs – a huge exhibition held annually by The Kennel Club which showcases every type of dog with a view to owning. (If you ever decide to go don't wear high heels or black clothes)

You get to ask dog-owners important questions about the different breeds in order to make the best choice for you. My questions consisted of *'Are they ok with noise?', 'Do they need a lot of walking or grooming?'* and *'Can they balance lemon slices on their nose while I do a tequila shot?'* They were slightly concerned about us being responsible enough and we were slightly concerned by the helpful terrier owner who cheerfully informed us that his breed were lovely dogs because *'if you were having a bit of a knock about with the wife the dog would stand up for her'*. We moved swiftly on...

Seeing all of these animals did bring it home to me how much work would be involved, work and responsibility. Our lives would have to radically change. Was I ready to take the next step? I knew I wasn't ready to do it alone, which means my relationship with Patrick came under the spotlight.

We had to ask ourselves if we were really ready to commit, not just to a dog, but to each other?

I've had a varied love life and can mentally cross of most of the major milestones you feel you should experience. I've had my heart broken (spending the subsequent year drunk), broken a few hearts myself, met a stranger off the internet, had an affair, been with a bad boy, been swept off my feet, been a friend with benefits and been happily single. But what did I want now? Did I really only want sex and fun? I had promised myself at least a year of doing nothing but dating and enjoying myself, being free of relationships and responsibility but here I was considering a new long term partner and a dog. I wanted to continue dining out in beautiful London restaurants, dressing up for industry parties and staying out late in Soho drinking dens. I didn't want to have leave early to get home and feed the dog.

But Patrick was serious about me and he didn't want to have just sex and fun. He wanted the whole thing. Could I risk losing him because I wanted the opportunity to have another year of being single? I knew I wasn't getting any younger and chances like the one I was being offered didn't come along every day. He went to Cuba for a few weeks to give me some time to think about things. But he left a present in my bedroom to help me make up my mind – the keys to his Porsche attached to a Tiffany bracelet. Smooth.

A very good friend of mine once gave me some wonderful advice, many years previously we had been bemoaning our single status and I confessed I was worried I would never find a guy willing to take on all of my baggage. Sagely she told me that one day I would meet someone who would not only take on all of my baggage but help me unpack it too, and that would be the guy I should hold onto. Well Patrick was that unpacker. I didn't need to try and be interesting and exciting as I had in previous relationship, I didn't need to try and be someone else. I decided to take the plunge.

Not without some regret I packed up my little single girl's flat and we moved in together. However, we were based in Camden - not far from central London life – and were still partying pretty much every night and sleeping in late at the weekends. It wasn't a home life conducive to owning a puppy.

It was time for a bit of an awakening. We realised that maybe we were getting a bit too old to go out as much as we were. Our hangovers were lasting longer and I noticed that the industry I worked in was getting younger and younger. My peers were pretty much all paired off: some were even considering (shock, horror) having a family! I had a fear of becoming the oldest swinger in town. I had terrible visions of trying to squeeze my now over 30 body into the latest fashions and stay out as late as these twenty-something girls I now saw at every event I went to (when I obviously couldn't do either as well as I used to).

I was reminded of a story concerning two women I used to work with. On entering the ladies toilet a friend of mine discovered our colleague admiring herself and her rather outrageous (far too young for her) outfit in the mirror. She was saying to herself *"Not bad for 45"*. My friend was incredulous and couldn't help herself asking "*What? That outfit only cost 45 pounds*?" Quick as a flash the pertinent response was: "*No, I'm 45, this dress cost hundreds*". Sadly we all knew that she probably wasn't that young and the horrible dress certainly wasn't worth more than £45 (even if it had cost a fortune). Would that be me in the future? Still trying to hang on to my youth and failing and making a fool of myself?

Maybe I did need a new focus? Patrick is nearly ten years older than me and I knew he felt that some settling down might be in order too. A dog would give us that focus, if we could look after a dog satisfactorily, learn to love it and look after it maybe we could see our way clear to being together forever and having our own family? Isn't that what everyone else did when they met the right person?

The search for our very own dog was on…

Chapter 2: THE PICKING OF A PUP

When you've spent years as a virtually lawless, single girl about town the idea of getting of a dog is a definite gear change, and a very obvious one. Everyone had a comment to make: *'it'll never last'*, *'that poor dog, he'll have to be taken out for walks you know?'* and *'does Soho House let dogs in?'*. And I got plenty of *'I assume you'll be getting a Chihuahua, or one of those handbag dogs?'* But despite the disparaging remarks, and my own reservations about my social life being over, we ploughed ahead with our search for the perfect pooch.

I had lots of literature we'd picked up from Discover Dogs and the internet is a great resource for choosing a suitable dog. Suitable: meaning one that will seamlessly fit into your life and require little change on your part. (Who am I kidding?)

After plenty of discussion we settled on a Staffordshire Bull Terrier for the following reasons:

1. Reasonably small but not so small Patrick would be embarrassed walking him and I

could probably dress him up and pick him up if I wanted to

2. Short coat which needs little upkeep
3. Playful (Patrick wanted a dog he could play ball with)
4. Affectionate without craving attention
5. Doesn't need to run for hours a day

All good. We did discuss Boxer dogs because my family had traditionally kept them (my grandparents once owned a Boxer bitch they called Bonnie because she was so ugly) but we dismissed them on account of the drool, their size, the amount of exercise and attention they need and the general over the top bounciness. I knew I was going to have to take the dog in to the office most days of the week (the joy of owning your own company) and I couldn't have a slathering beast running riot and grinning and gurning at everyone while we were trying to work. At this point yes, I was still trying to find the dog that would slot perfectly into our lives as they were right then.

Then one morning I got a phone call, it was Patrick:

"We're definitely getting a Boxer".

"Oh, are we? Why?"

"I've just met the most gorgeous one in the street, we have to have one, she kissed me and she wasn't drooly", he replied excitedly.

The fact he had been kissed by a friendly dog wasn't a reason to change our plans, was it? Well we'd both been quite impetuous in our lives so maybe we should consider it. They certainly looked a bit more unusual than a Staffie (sorry to lovers of that beautiful, misunderstood breed) and I could probably cope with the larger size for an increase in dog status. I believed that a Boxer had more show-off points than perhaps a smaller breed. Oh dear, was it time to question our reasons for getting a dog again?

Once again we turned to the internet and found some accredited breeders with new puppies. We knew we wanted a male dog. Well, I did. Patrick would have loved a little princess bitch but I was adamant – there was only one princess in the house and that was me!

We made a few speculative phone calls. One woman put the phone down on me the second I told her we lived in London. She wouldn't even consider letting us see her litter. I hadn't even started on my spiel about being in a stable relationship, having a garden and spacious flat, being able to take our new dog to work so he wouldn't be left alone for hours, blah blah blah. Disheartened I left a few messages here and there and thought no more about it.

My 33rd birthday was coming up and we were planning a party. I had one every year, I like to mark the passing of time. The year before had been fantastic, Patrick and I had got together that very night and so it was also our one year anniversary coming up, (something to celebrate indeed). Thoughts of getting a dog were pushed to the back of my mind. Maybe I believed it never would really happen.

Then, two weeks before my birthday I received a phone call from a farm in Northamptonshire. They had one male pup left. He was a brindle, which essentially means stripy, with little white socks. Now I had my heart set on a red coloured dog as I wasn't a fan of brindle but that heart started beating a little faster and I immediately called Patrick:

"*We need to go to Northamptonshire tomorrow there's a puppy he's the only one left he has small white socks and we need to go and see him tomorrow before he goes he's in Northamptonshire which isn't very far I know he's a brindle and I didn't want a brindle really but we should go and see him anyway*" I garbled down the phone without pausing for breath.

"*Calm down. Don't get your hopes up. You are not meant to buy the first puppy you see!*" The voice of reason explained.

"*Of course we can go and see him if you like but there is no way you will come home with him, so what's the point? Maybe we should continue to wait for more suitable pups closer to home?*"

I took a breath. Of course he was right. If I was prepared to hold on a red Boxer pup would turn up eventually closer to home. We decided to wait.

So the next morning we found ourselves motoring up the M1 on our way to Northamptonshire, grinning madly. We talked in the car about my impending birthday celebrations and how there was no way we would be able to pick up a puppy today because we both needed to go to the party – we had joint friends by now and it wasn't only my birthday but our first anniversary. No, we couldn't have a puppy now, it just wasn't practical, it certainly didn't fit into our immediate social diary.

We drove the Porsche, a lovely sporty, black convertible (a Boxster funnily enough) and caused a bit of a stir as we pulled into the drive alongside the huge farm vehicles. I'm sure the couple who made their way towards us clocked us as 'city types', but they welcomed us in.

We were led to a caravan on site and inside we found a few puppies rolling around on the floor with some children. Everyone was chewing everyone else and hair and fur were flying. I almost shuddered as I breathed in the hairy air and imagined the state of my clothes as I gingerly sat down to discuss the puppies.

"*This one's yours*" said the woman, and she pulled a tiny scrap of furry bones out of the melee and handed it to me. Something warm and smelly and scratchy struggled against my chest for two seconds before relaunching itself into the skirmish on the floor and skittering away.

"*He's a littl'un sadly, his sisters took all the milk and food, so he's not really grown a lot*" she continued. "*He also likes biting hair*"
Looking closer it was obvious the darkest pup was smaller than the rest of the larger red bitches who were decidedly chunky. I immediately felt sorry for this little brave boy, belittled and bullied by his sisters, but gamely playing on in what amounted to a continuous canine affray.
"*His kennel name is Fletch's Flyer*" she continued. Yes well, that would have to change, I thought.

Patrick was standing in the corner, and despite the almost visible shake of the head and disapproving look I knew he wouldn't be able to leave him behind either. We were falling prey to everything you are told not to – don't feel sorry for the puppy, don't go for the smallest one, don't take the first one you see.

I tried to regain control of the situation.
"Can we see his mother?" I asked. I knew this to be an important part of the process and although I wasn't sure what it was meant to achieve I was proud of myself. The woman shrugged but agreed, she obviously didn't know what it would achieve either. We were led to some grassland. I was rather disgruntled as I was wearing new ballet pumps and hadn't counted on stomping through muddy fields.

Behind a barbed wire fence were two completely different dogs, a big grey one and a small black one. The grey was incredibly large and scary looking, as he eyed us up and curled his lip we were thankful for the fencing between us. His huge wet chops hung down glistening with drool and anger.

"That must be Dad" I said unhelpfully. *"He's a big boy"*

Patrick nervously gripped my shoulders, I could tell he was inches away from yanking me out of the mud and back into the car and civilisation. Next to Dad was a small, squat bitch who looked sadly through the wire at us. Maybe she knew we had come to take one of her offspring, maybe she was just miserable at having Brute as her mate? I would have been if I had been her.

"They've both got Crufts winners in their bloodline" we were informed pleasantly by our host. I couldn't imagine anything further from that glamorous dog event than this windswept joyless field but I nodded in agreement. In fact, I couldn't imagine anything more miserable than living on this cold farm, but that's just me.

"OK we'll take him" Before the words were out of my mouth I knew it was a mistake but that was it, he was ours and the sooner we got him out of there and home the better. I was worried about what would happen to a worthless runt on a farm in middle-England and thought he would enjoy his life far better in our comfortable home than being bullied in

that caravan. I knew Patrick was in agreement, I just knew it.

We scooped up this little scrap of puppy, were given some certificates, a bag of feed and a little basket for him to travel home in, and after hastily dashing off a cheque for a large amount of money in return, we were off. What had we done? What indeed? I had a birthday party coming up! And I was willing to bet that the bar I had booked didn't allow dogs in? But it was too late now, we were suddenly dog owners...

THE FIRST PICTURE!

Chapter 3: THE SHOCK OF THE NEW

The thing about having a dog, as opposed to any other animal, is that it highlights what you have that others (especially if you live in London) might not – such as a garden, larger accommodation, a live in partner, time and money on your hands and the possibility of a family in your near future. It's like the first rung on the ladder of that elusive status – being settled. So were we settled? Not for a long time.

After whining at being separated from his family, and being sick on the beautiful cream leather interior (it was his first journey in a car after all) our new pup eventually curled into a tiny ball in my lap and fell into a restless sleep. Our drive home was fraught, full of recriminations at our actions but also full of delight at this living creature cradled in my arms. It was a huge rush and mixture of emotions, we kept smiling at each other but not sure of the consequences of what we had done. Was our home ready? Were *we* ready? Could we keep him alive?

"Well, that's it. We've done it now" said Patrick. *"We'll need to pick up some food and call the vets straight away"*

"Why?" I answered. *"What's the matter with him?"* Had Patrick's eagle eyes spotted some problem that I hadn't?

"Probably nothing but we need to get him registered and he'll need various puppy pills and injections".

Oh and so here it was, the mundane, the problems, the logistics, the normality and every day of pet ownership. The important things that I put to the back of my mind when I imagined my dog and I frolicking in a sunny park or strolling around Primrose Hill looking for a spot for lunch. I really needed to grow up and get a grip of reality! Patrick smiled at me, maybe he thought it was time I needed to grow up too and what was snoozing in my lap was going to help me do it. He leant over to stroke the top of the pup's head and then he stroked mine too. Thankfully I wouldn't need to do it alone.

We tried to introduce our gangly, new charge gently to his new home. I carried him in and kept him on my lap with some cloth we had taken from the farm that would smell familiar (which meant terrible). He kept whining. I imagine he felt very lonely, even though his sisters seemed like mean bitches they were the only family he had and I am sure he was wondering where they were.

When he was put on the floor he immediately had a wee, which we expected, that was fine. In fact he couldn't take more than a few steps without having a wee. He also couldn't take more than a few steps without having a little sleep. He was largely uninterested in food. His tiny legs were as slim as pencils and he smelt awful. We hovered round him like buzzing parental flies trying to ascertain his every need, before he even knew what it was.

The three of us spent our first nervous night under the same roof together and I don't think any of us got any decent sleep. Puppy slept huddled between us, with all of us waking every hour as he whimpered and scrabbled around. This wouldn't do at all.

The next day we bought him his own little bed – a soft brown corduroy pouch that fitted in with our bedroom décor brilliantly. But after many nights of me trying to sleep with one foot hanging out of my bed and into his (so he had something warm and alive to sleep up against) he was still crying and fretting. Our new dog obviously hated sleeping alone. He was eventually hoisted back onto the bed between us and where that dog sleeps is still a bone of contention in our home to this day!

When a puppy is that young, ours was just 12 weeks old when we picked him up, they can't be left alone. Also, and I hadn't known this before (talk about going in with your eyes open) they can't step out on public ground before they have had their final puppy jabs in case of disease. Which meant we had to go through two months of carrying and driving him everywhere. So Patrick and I were on constant pup-sitting duty.

There wasn't a moment when one of us couldn't be indoors with him and we began to feel the strain almost immediately as we tried to divide up the normal tasks of food shopping and going to work. Forget about going out for drinks!

As he was unable to go on the bus to work we started racking up huge costs in those first few months on the congestion charge for driving the three of us into central London and parking in Soho every day. And if you have ever negotiated the roads through the Capital during rush hour you will know just how much this stressed us out having to drive in every day.

But the strain just wasn't financial. We were used to our freedom and being able to do whatever we wanted whenever we wanted and had never even really checked in with each other. Now our lives were all about plans and timetables and organising ourselves so that someone was on dog duty at all times, it was rather like military planning, taking both jobs and the car into account. I felt myself wanting to rebel already , in my head I was positive that although having a dog was going to change my life it wasn't going to change my lifestyle, which was incredibly naïve of me. I set about planning my birthday party again knowing full well that Patrick wouldn't be able to attend now, but as long as I could still go out then I'd know little had changed.

The big night dawned and I met my usual crowd in a lovely Soho bar. I was dressed up, I was in heels, I had checked myself for dog hair and I didn't smell of wee. The cocktails started lining the bar and life was good. Most people wanted to ask questions about our new acquisition but conversation quickly moved on to more gossipy topics, work, friends and the like, everything I normally liked discussing. But I found I wanted to extend the conversations about the puppy, I kept showing off little pictures I had of his tiny face on my mobile phone, even to the barman at one stage. I imagined Patrick at home playing with him, cuddling him and eventually getting into bed and I knew I would rather be at home. I even turned to one of my best friends and howled *"I can't believe I am here with you when I could be at home with my dog"*. Things had definitely changed whether I liked it or not. Or had I changed? Whatever, the party was most definitely over and we all headed home before midnight. Unheard of.

Having a tiny scrap of a pup around the home was suddenly delightful and his little ways and exploits where hysterical to us. We have hundreds of photos of him from this time he was so small and cute. But he was so small that I lost him in the house one day. I couldn't find him anywhere. I raced around calling to him and looking in cupboards, running up and down the stairs. In my panic I nearly slipped on a pile of washing that was sitting on the bottom step, this toppling of clothes revealed a tiny puppet face nestling in amongst the knickers, he had burrowed into the clean laundry and I had nearly stomped on him!

The battle to ease our young charge into his new surroundings continued and he soon regained some of the early spark that we had seen in the chaotic caravan of his birth (he even started chewing my hair which I took as a good sign). Maybe he would start to think of this as his home and us as his parents? Patrick and I certainly now considered ourselves as such. We were also engaged to be married...

Chapter 4: THE POWER OF A NAME

Our new pup had been with us for about four days before we managed to settle on a name for him. It was a difficult and drawn out process and very similar to, and as important as, naming a child. After dismissing my original suggestion of TIGER (on account of his fetching red and black stripe effect) for sounding too much like something Jamie Oliver would name a kid, we bought a Baby Names book to look for ideas.

As the book contained around 4,000 names I suggested our choice should begin with the letter B, as he was a Boxer, to help narrow the field. I favoured BARCLAY and BUSTER both dismissed by Patrick, (who had no suggestions of his own to offer). Giving it up as a hopeless task I was relieved to come home from work on the fourth day to find that the pup finally had a name and there was no argument to be had about it.

"He's called BASIL" offered Patrick as soon as I walked through the door. So why was this a fait accompli?

"He told me that was his name..."

OK then. And that was that. Basil it was!

Trainers and dog lovers cannot stress the importance enough of your dog learning its name. This is so they can respond to commands and come back to you when you call. We took this very seriously and can confirm that, to date, Basil has been called by only about 20 or so names. The list includes – but is not exclusive to – the below:

- Pup Pup
- Puppetty
- Officer Nibble (for obvious reasons)
- Poo Bear
- Bassie Booboos
- Boobeus Dogrid (a nod to Harry Potter)
- Whoopit
- Bizness Bazness
- Doggie Dudes
- Billy Bollocks

- Basil W. Barksworth (the W stands for a very rude word)
- Puglyig
- Charlie Cairoli (because he acts like a clown)
- Baby Bas
- Sir Stinksalot (after a fart)
- Dumpling Dog
- Doctor Bas (he takes a lot of interest in the putting on of plasters and the cutting of toenails)

My friends call him 'the Brown Lamb' for some reason.

His plethora of names started to lend themselves to little jingles and tunes. Many sing to their babies but we soon found ourselves singing to our dog! In fact we now have a bit of a repertoire of songs or *Odes to Basil*. We take variations of his name and incorporate them into different musical numbers such as *The Sand Dance, Xanadu, Agadoo* or the *EastEnders* theme tune.

Sometimes when I am away from Basil I sing one of his little songs to make myself feel closer to him. I remember the night before my wedding I was having dinner in Knightsbridge with my two best friends – a kind of last glamorous, girly night out before the first one of us got hitched. We had dropped Basil off that morning at his 'dog hotel' to look after him while we were on our honeymoon and as I was feeling a bit emotional I unconsciously started humming a Basil tune. When I explained what I was doing my friends were delighted. Screaming with mirth they made me take them through some of our favourite songs and fuelled by rather a lot of wine, I obliged. Even now when we are out it comes up and I am asked to do a rendition of the latest Basil song!

Patrick and I began to call ourselves Mummy and Daddy, which I know sounds ridiculous and is usually only the premise of long married couples with a huge brood of children but we liked it. (Obviously we only did it within the safety of our own home).

Chapter 5: THE NINE TO FIVE

It was always agreed that in order to have a dog I would have to take him into my office on days I was working so that he wasn't left alone for any length of time, especially when he was a young pup. So armed with a huge bag of puppy essentials and a new bed Basil got ready for his first day in the office. I was even planning on him having his own email address and a spot on the Company website. He also had a calendar of visits planned from new friends desperate to come up and pay him a visit and bring little 'Welcome to Soho' gifts. But it wasn't all fun and games, certainly not at first.

I found the emotional responsibility of having Basil with me every moment of the day, unable to let him out of my sight and having to pick him up even to go out of the door, while trying to continue my day to day work rather wearing. I was used to popping out for a coffee with colleagues, enjoying long boozy lunches or arranging impromptu drinks after work whenever I felt like it. I lost count of the times I texted or called friends to meet them as usual before suddenly remembering I couldn't and cancelling. I would then spend the evening imagining all sorts of high jinks happening around Soho without me and feel miserable.

I was a member of a very expensive and exclusive Soho gym that I loved. I usually only went to use the steam room and have a cold shower when I was very hungover but I still missed it. Not being able to use it made me want to go more. You'd have thought I was a dedicated gym bunny the way I complained about not being able to go every lunchtime.

Patrick and I found ourselves arguing quite a lot during this period and I was desperate for the days he could get off work so I could go into the office on my own knowing Basil was being looked after at home. Those days I had 'off duty' I really let my hair down and furiously arranged various social engagements, which wasn't perhaps the best response to having a new, needy charge who depended on me at home. But the adjustment to the responsibility of owning a dog was a big one and I really needed to let go now and again to remember what my life was like BB (Before Basil). Funnily enough the rare occasions I did manage to get out I would spend a huge amount of time talking about the little pup and missing him dreadfully.

These days seemed to drag on interminably and it seemed that we would be chained together forever. Patrick and I took to eating gorgeous meals and drinking champagne at home to try and recreate our previous glamorous lives without leaving the flat, and I found that for the first time in years I had to have a relatively clear diary. If we went out in the evening it had to be without the other, which was another test for our relationship. It wasn't until he was a few months older that we felt we could leave him alone in the flat and soon instigated a regular Saturday night 'date-night' just to try and bring some romance back into our relationship. We would give ourselves a couple of hours out of the house to discover a local bar or restaurant without having to check if they allowed dogs in first. Like any other nervous parents we would usually spend the evening talking about Basil or fretting about him but without a babysitter to ring up and check in with.

But most evenings the three of us would sit on the sofa, Basil between Patrick and I with both of us holding a paw each, watching TV or chatting. We became very affectionate and tactile with each other and still are, Basil absolutely adores a cuddle. So when I am too busy for a stroke and push Basil away Patrick will now remark *"You weren't like that when we were playing tiddlywinks earlier"*, a reference from Basil's namesake, Basil Brush. Tiddlywinks is now a euphemism for a having a cuddle in our house, or the delicious occasions when Basil tries to nibble your ears.

A dog in a family home can be a terrible 'affection Hoover' - sucking up all of the attention and cuddles on offer leaving very little for anyone else. But they are also a fantastic 'row diffuser', it is very hard to carry on being angry with your partner when you have a beloved pet in common.

While I was bemoaning the change in my lifestyle I was also secretly relishing how Basil had set about charming everyone in the office. On his first day it took quite a while for everyone to realise he was actually there – he had curled up on me and was sleeping when the team started arriving. He was so small he could fit under the desk while on my lap! I soon started beckoning people over to get a look at the tiny puppy that could fit in one of my hands and that was soon to become part of their working lives.

Everyone was delighted at how absolutely gorgeous he was (something I tried to remind them all about later when he started weeing in their handbags, jumping up at their fragile, diaphanous skirts and eating their sandwiches). Mobile phones were out, photos or videos were taken and texted around London – *'our new team member'*.

Because he was too young to be toilet trained outdoors I attempted to coach him in using training pads in the office – large squares of nappy like material that absorb doggy dos and wees – and a couple of these were religiously laid out in the same spots in the office every morning. And every day the young Basil ignored them and did his business wherever he could get into, usually under a table or desk, or hidden behind a cupboard, meaning I had to hunt around for them. Because he was so small he had a tiny capacity to hold anything in and usually weed and pooed every hour, I was forever jumping up and down with poobags, sprays and wipes instead of getting on with my work.

In order to train your young pup you are meant to keep an eye on their behaviour so you can recognise the signs they are about to go to the loo and direct them to a more appropriate spot, hoping they would go there naturally the next time. Sadly I couldn't keep an eye on Basil all the time while I was working and usually the first I knew that he had gone again was when a cry would go up somewhere in the office of *'Oh Basil'*. He took to hiding in tiny areas and often a smell would alert us to the fact a poo was hidden behind a door or in a cupboard. Thankfully the office had a wooden floor.

Sometimes - just by chance - his little deposits or puddles would be on or near the training mats, which would prompt me to show them to the office and exclaim: *'Look! He's learning. He's really close to it. Oh well done Basil!'* Regrettably sometimes an unsuspecting team member would tread in a Basil poo, and I would feel terrible as I saw the soft package squelch up between Havaianas clad toes. As I say it was a difficult time, and obviously not just for me.

One time he bought us perilously close to a serious brush with the law! Basil had his dog bowls of food and water next to my desk. In the evening I would throw that day's water out of the window – we were four floors up above Wardour Street and I figured it wouldn't do much harm. One night we were packing up to go home and I did my usual flinging out of the window, within three minutes a panting red-faced man arrived at our door, obviously having flown up the many flights of stairs to our lofty abode.

"Did someone from in here just throw some water out of the window?" he asked angrily. Everyone looked

nervously between the open window and the empty dog bowl on my desk.

"No" I lied. *"Why?"*

He turned around – his leather jacket was covered in it, as was the back of his head.

"Some has just landed on me, I was standing directly outside your building and it obviously came from above"

He was getting redder and redder.

"Oh no, what a shame" I was all concern. *"What are you going to do?"*

"Well, I'm a policeman and I am going to find those who did it" he vowed.

Leaving his card he suggested we get in touch if we found anything out and we nodded mutely. He raced off to check with every other office in the building and we hastily shut up the office and bundled Basil off into the early evening air.

Basil became part of our working life and everyone got used to finding dog treats in the biscuit barrel or their lunch missing. The office smelt of dried liver chunks and we became quite adept at explaining to phoning clients what that barking was in the background. He ended up having his own Facebook and MySpace pages and even his own office email address. He was close to going on the payroll.

GETTING READY FOR WORK

Chapter 6: THE TRICK WITH TRAINING

Housetraining a dog is a difficult process, I don't care how many trainers or well-meaning owners tell you otherwise. Everyone has a theory or a method and let me tell you they are all rubbish, especially if your dog has other ideas. There are no quick ways of doing it, it's all trial and error and time! We tried the carefully laid out bits of newspaper, the clicker commands, the designated wee spot etc etc but Basil ploughed his own furrow and weed wherever he liked. He hated newspaper.

The challenge was to get him to use the dog flap Patrick had installed in the back door and do his business outside in our small garden. But the flap was scary, it made a clapping noise and rattled in the wind. Basil was suspicious. And I was getting bored of mopping up wee and picking up poo.

I can't even begin to remember the amount of times I sat crouched on the floor cooing at a shivering Basil who obviously desperate for a wee would run away and hide rather than go through the charade of me trying to tempt him outside with a treat while holding the flap open. Eventually we started following him around the house and every time he started to go we would pick him up and push him through the flap. He would indignantly stand there looking at us through the glass door, his flow completely stopped, and wait for us to let him back in again so he could finish off what he had started indoors.

He just loved doing his business in the house. Even when we took him for a walk he would wait until the second we were back in the front door before going. We could stay out for hours and we did sometimes just desperate for him to go outside so that we could praise his behaviour and show him that that was where you were meant to go. But, oh no, he could hold it in for ages if it meant he could have a wee or poo in the safety of his own home. When he finally did pluck up enough courage to 'go' outside of the house, he still had to kind of be 'indoors' and so ended up weeing on the bus, in the pub, in the car, on neighbour's doorsteps and once memorably on Patrick's head as he was lifting him up.

Eventually the message started getting through. And after a lot of trial and error Basil started hesitantly sniffing the flap to the garden, gingerly poking his nose through it, followed by his head, Patrick and I hovered in the background trying not to make a sound or a fuss. But we nearly exploded with joy the first time he hopped through the flap and triumphantly had a wee outside without our help. He didn't even seem to mind the flaps clapping noise.

The sound of the dog flap is a welcome one in our house. At night we still listen out as soon as Basil starts making his way downstairs, the tension is palpable. Will he use it? Will he go outside? Will there be a little poo present waiting for us in the lounge in the morning? Ah, and there goes the clapping sound, success! Good boy.

But getting the dog house trained is not the end of the wee story I'm afraid! Yes Basil did learn to wee outside and we were all grateful but our fight continues – not over where he does it but how he does it. We were and still are desperate for him to cock his leg properly like a boy dog, however, because we had him castrated before he learnt there is a danger he might never get to grips with the 'proper' way to wee.

He doesn't even squat like a girl so we can pretend he's a bitch, it's more of a stretch forward, the angle of which means he invariably ends up weeing on his front paws. In the early days, when he was a lot shorter, one of his white socks went a bit yellow. We call these PeePaws – it's how you can tell Basil has had a wee, either by a trail of fetching little paw prints on the pavement or a damp paw in your lap! It's a lottery if you go to hold him by the paws if you are going to get a wet one or not. And never stand downwind of him if he is having a little tinkle as you'll end up with a spray all over your legs, so aimless is his direction.

He does sniff the right kind of things before weeing, like telegraph poles and the like, but still doesn't naturally make the leap to actually lifting his leg. I used to creep up behind him while he was weeing and try and lift his leg up for him with my foot hoping he would get the idea. After about the tenth time of him running off without finishing his wee and starting to look warily at me every time he wanted to go I realised I might be giving him a complex and stopped.

Sometimes a natural instinct takes over and he does cock his leg – there is no rhyme or reason for this and is usually a cause for great celebration and congratulations, much to Basil's bemusement. I remember the first time his lovely dog walker witnessed such an event and sent me the following text: *'Great day - this is the first time I have seen Basil do a big dog wee!'*

I always used to say in a sing-song type voice *'Wee Wee'* whenever he went, to try and give the action some kind of command as I heard it helped with toilet training. I still used to do it almost out of habit, until recently, when Basil looked at me witheringly as if to say *'I'm not a puppy'*.

Chapter 7: THE PROBLEM WITH POO

As this is a book about a dog we have to address the fact that he doesn't only wee. He also poos. And so, what follows are some thoughts and stories about poo! Some of it might be too much information (well it is about defecation). Sorry.

But let's start with a funny poo story before we get into the real sticky stuff...

Basil needs to keep an eye on you when he is crouching to do his business, he can be a bit sensitive and maybe he feels vulnerable whilst he is in such a position? I don't know. Anyway, Patrick was out having a late night trot around the block with the boy when he started to turn his familiar, crouching circle in front of a parked black taxi. As soon as Basil got going the door of a nearby house opened up and a glamorous couple comprising of a well-known film and TV actor and his equally famous girlfriend (who lived in the cobbled street behind our house) came out and got into the cab without seeing what was squatted in the dark in front of it.

The cab flicked on its headlights to reveal a crouching Basil directly in front of them and barring their way. He was trying to evacuate what turned out to be a particularly hard to shift poo, brightly lit up in all his shaking glory and staring sadly and desperately at his Dad. For what seemed like an eternity Basil anxiously tried to go about his business while Patrick hopped from one foot to another willing him to finish, with this illustrious audience staring out at him from the cab, obviously keen to be on their way but unable to drive down the narrow street.

Eventually, business done, Patrick stepped up to clean up the poo - which of course was now all between the cobbles - and with a nod and a shrug to the cab to show that he had finished they were finally off. I am sure they will never remember the sight of our poor dog picked out in their headlights and holding up their cab, but I know my husband will never forget it.

I saw the aforementioned actor at an awards ceremony a few months later and in a drunken moment thought seriously about going up to him and asking if he remembered it and to introduce myself as the dog's mother and apologise. I thought we might be able to have a chummy laugh about it, maybe end up becoming friends, invite each other to neighbourly dinner parties, that kind of thing. Thankfully sanity prevailed and I steered clear of him. He is now one of the most popular UK actors working in Hollywood and his wife stars in the biggest UK film franchise ever. We will be reminded of Basil's 'incident' forever!

Picking up poo is a minefield (hopefully not literally) – there are many things to consider and remember. Never ever forget your poobags! I have had many a nervous journey across town without a bag on me, hurrying Basil along until we get to the safety of home and garden, and I have actually dragged him away from a few potential poo crouches because I didn't have a bag on me. *'Suck it back up boy'*

The reasons for picking up poo are twofold – you don't want to leave the unhygienic, smelly things lying around for others to step in (for those of us who have stepped in dog poo wearing high heeled sandals, you know the kind of bad karma you wish on those who left it there? Well I don't want that on my head). But also it's hard to take the shame when you are given dirty looks by those who see you leaving those little pavement presents behind. I would much prefer to take the embarrassment of stooping down to pick up than look like an uncaring cow with no thought of keeping the streets clean. If he does manage to squeeze one out while I am without a poobag, I will make a big show of looking for one in my pockets with over elaborate shoulder shrugs to make it clear to anyone watching that I usually do have them on me. Honest.

Most people pop the scooped poop back into their handbags or pockets, I just can't bring myself to put the little bags into my handbag now. I used to, but gave up when I got my first Marc Jacobs, there was something sacrilegious about it, I just couldn't. I didn't mind people seeing the tell-tale black poobag in the one hand, as long as the new leather tote was clean and pristine in the other. Even the best tied up poobag could always spell danger and MJ doesn't deserve that. And the new Burberry hasn't even been seen by the dog let alone been taken out on a walk.

You see the danger of not carrying a used poobag in your hand until you find a bin to put it in is that you might just forget that you have stashed it somewhere. So the next time you start rummaging around your handbag or pocket you could end up clasping your fingers around a forgotten, old bag of poo. Or imagine if one had leaked? It has happened!

So, remember your poobags! But if you don't have any on you when out with the dog keep an eye out for handy carrier bags or discarded crisp packets – anything – just don't get caught short. I sometimes forget to top up my handbag or just expect my husband to have some on him (which should never be done). But I soon learnt the importance of making sure I had something suitable with me... The hard way.

One evening Basil started his familiar circling just outside a packed Soho pub on the way home. It was sunny and the streets were thronged with happy after-work drinkers. Quite alone, a fear gripped me as I knew I didn't have any bags. Thrilled to see a squatting dog the drinkers decided to serenade us both with fun, loud songs about dogs and generally cheering on the poo process, ensuring that everyone in that busy street knew that my dog was doing his business!

After depositing a sizeable amount on the street Basil started skipping around on the end of his lead and putting on a show. I was reaching desperately around in my handbag for anything that would suffice (and once you start looking like you are going to pick up you can't just give it up as a bad job half way through and walk off because that's even more embarrassing) eventually I found a tissue. It tried valiantly to do the job but it just wasn't designed for such a purpose. It managed about half, the rest I had to do by hand. Eventually even the singing drinkers had to turn away as I helplessly mopped the pavement with the useless bit of thin, ripped paper...

Without going into too much detail I sat on the bus on the way home with tears in my eyes and some scrapings of Basil's deposits under my fingernails. I really love my dog but some days that love is tested.

Basil, like many canines, once he has evacuated his bowels loves to just skip around to celebrate the fact. He goes into a kind of ecstasy! As soon as the last little bit hits the tarmac Basil makes it his mission to get as far away from the pile as soon as possible and make as many leaps and spins as he can while doing it. Sadly it means that while you are trying to pick it up he is pulling you around in his attempts to get away. It makes life as a responsible dog owner very difficult and now I usually wait for the first flush of excitement to die down before I bend down, or take him off his lead which means you have to keep one eye on him to check he isn't running away and one eye on the poo.

But please never attempt to copy the time I decided to cut out the middle man (the road) and get Basil to go directly into a bag. One day he was taking a bit of time to do his business and as I stood behind him with a poobag ready I had a thought – why not open the bag up under him so the poo goes straight in? No picking it up off the floor, what a great idea. I crouched behind my crouching dog and as I waited for the poo to drop into my ready bag Basil became so freaked out at my proximity he bunny-hopped away from me still in the poo position. As I reached forward to try and catch his efforts I fell forward placing my hands straight in it as Basil ran away leaving loads of little dollops behind him. So not only did I now have to pick up lots of poos but my hands were covered in it. Maybe not the best idea I have ever had?

I have plenty of terrible poo stories (such as the £2 coin that fell out of my purse and rolled down the road and into a new wet one – what are the chances?) and I won't go into all of them here, but a friend of mine has a good one: while walking her dog in the dark she bent down and wrapped the bag around a cold, hard lump. Now there are many horrid things that can happen when you are dealing with poo (see above) but picking up an unknown dog's cold, old poo? That's just the worst!

A couple more essential things you need to know before you stoop to scoop the poop (and you surely don't need me to explain the reasons why but believe me I've learnt from personal experience):

- never wear a lovely long fringed scarf on a dog walk, certainly never anything made from trailing (unwashable and expensive) cashmere
- always put your gloves, phone, keys, purse, dog lead in your pocket before you bend down, never just hold loosely in your hand. You don't want to be picking any of those out of a freshly laid turd
- take your heavy shoulder bag off beforehand, otherwise it will swing right into that poo
- if it's a particularly windy day then make sure you have hold of that poobag securely before you go to grip the mess - you really don't want

the bag blowing off down the street before you close your fingers together

- If your dog has diarrhoea then it is best to just walk away, I know it's terrible but there is nothing you can do about liquid poo. I once tried to unsuccessfully scrape some up with a carrier bag but just smeared it all over the pavement. I can only suggest you stand well clear (it's hell to get out of suede) and try to position your dog over a drain if at all possible. Otherwise just hold your head up high, walk on and pray for rain

But it's not all bad. My husband makes the best of it by describing the plastic bags filled with fresh poo as *'little hand warmers'* perfect for keeping your fingers nice and toasty - ok on a cold day, not so nice on a hot one.

There is also something empowering about holding a bag of dog poo. Especially walking around some areas of North London, there are lots of scary people about and dog theft rates are rising all the time. I feel that even those who wouldn't be scared by me approaching with a knife or weapon of any sort (as they probably had their own) would run if faced with a flying open bag of fresh doggy do. Like most dog owners both me and my husband would resort to any measure to protect our boy from dog-nappers. It's just something comforting to hold on to while walking the dog late at night!

Another thing I have started thinking about on dog walks concerns poo I see on the street. Yes sadly not everyone goes to such lengths to ensure their dog's dinner is not left around for everyone to step in and I see a lot of it while walking about. In fact I can't ignore it now. After Basil's last tummy upset and an onslaught of the most terrible diarrhoea I became obsessed with him having good solid stools. But when I found myself looking at other dog's droppings and thinking: *now that's a good one, I wish Basil would do one that looked like that* I knew I had probably gone too far. I would like to think that there is at least one other dog owner in the world who has suffered 'turd envy', but I fear I may be the only one?

Chapter 8: THE IMPORTANCE OF A GOOD EDUCATION

People were keen to inform us that we had to *'get him trained'* and that *'a trained dog was a good dog'* etc, and as we were keen to be responsible owners we set about buying training manuals and DVDs (or got given them as presents). We had about four books by the bed at one point – and all of them had different techniques and opinions on dog-training. I got about half way through all of them. But not before trying out something from them all – and soon the bemused Basil was being shoved off the sofa, having his meals after ours, not being cuddled for days at a time, being ignored on arrival home and having endless commands barked at him in order to get him to sit, lie down, roll over and stay.

Patrick's response was that; while it was good he would obey us if we needed him to - if we had to dispense with cuddles, titbits from the table and joyous welcomes at the door, then what was the point of having a dog? Despite trying desperately to instil some puppy law and order in the house I had to kind of agree with him. And now my enduring image of Basil's response to this flurry of activity on the training front is a set of dusty books under the bed, all of which had been defiantly chewed – his own little toothy protest.

I'd seen a programme that showed how you could train your dog to jump through a hoop in just a few lessons. I eagerly purchased a hoop and after getting Basil used to it – at first he reacted like I had bought a nuclear warhead into the house – spent literally hours and hours and hours trying to teach him to launch himself spectacularly through the hoop held high in the air (while I imagined admiring friends watching wide eyed). He eventually managed to step through the hoop while I held it on the ground, and only after a huge amount of treats had been thrown through it. My dreams of a performing dog sadly, it seemed, were not going to come true. If anyone shouts '*jump*' near Basil (or a word that sounds even remotely like it) now he still looks round nervously to see if I am advancing on him with a large hoop.

One thing we did agree on was 'Puppy Classes'. We knew socialisation was important - mainly to boost his confidence - but also because I liked to think of it as a kind of finishing school for good dogs seeking an entrance into Society. Like a canine debutantes' ball! So we enrolled him in the weekly classes held at our local vets. This was an hourly session with a tough but fair trainer and a lovely veterinary nurse. It was a combination of the practical (training and socialising) and theory (questions and experience exchanging) and Basil and I loved them.

The best part was seeing Basil interact with other young puppies – and of course it was fun for me because who wouldn't enjoy spending an hour surrounded by gambolling pups? There was the hard, but pretty, Staffordshire Bull Terrier bitch, the aloof (owner too) pampered King Charles Spaniel, the massive, uncontrollable Alsatian (who had been puncturing his gentle owners arms) and the tiny French Bulldog with a patch over one eye, full of character and appropriately called Marcel who became a particular friend. Basil romped with all of them and I constantly filmed his efforts to make friends on my phone to send to Patrick (sometimes instead of listening to what was being taught). Of course it broke my heart when he was left out of a particularly fun wrestle or had been bested in fight – much like a mum watching her first born interacting at school. I actually found myself saying out loud: *'come on play nice'* as I tried to pull the rollicking pups apart. But it is all part of the puppy process of learning and growing up.

I was meant to be working from home at the same time as attending Puppy Classes and I could see the other attendees looking at me oddly as I set out my mobile phone and Blackberry on the table at the beginning of each lesson. It made me laugh sometimes that I was responding to an email about a particularly important matter while trying to entice Basil to come back at my call with a smelly liver treat.

Sometimes Patrick would drop in half way through if he could get away from work – just to see how the boy was doing – looking smart enough in a very casual room to prompt the trainer to quip *'ignore him, that's my lawyer here to discuss some owner complaints'.* Poor Basil would be so excited to see his dad his concentration would go right out of the window.

One particularly memorable lesson involved learning basic medical skills, to help your dog if he has been in an accident or became ill. Basil was chosen as the test dog to be bandaged up in front of the class. I knew it would be a disaster. And it was. After allowing the kindly vet nurse to get the bandages round his head (obviously under duress) he managed to get the end of it in his mouth and while she was tying up one end he was busy unwinding the other looking like a maniacal canine mummy. He was distraught at having a bandage wrapped around his paw and wouldn't sit still long enough to display how it was done. Soon he was off running around the room with bandages flying – like a medical version of the Andrex puppy.

We both learnt lots at our Puppy Classes and Basil soon grew in confidence on his walks and got used to people and other dogs. He still sits and lies down very nicely when asked and I still have a huge fondness for French Bulldogs.

A trained pet is a wonder! We share very little of the same gene pool and obviously don't speak the same language so I am constantly amazed that a dog will follow me around without a lead, come when called and sit when asked. I am sure that we are actually communicating or maybe it's just 'cupboard love'? I don't mind what is going on just as long as I look cool and in command as I wander around the neighbourhood with a compliant Basil trotting along behind me. And people will stop and stare when Patrick is controlling him with a toy ball, Basil will roll over, run and come back, sit down, stand up, make you a cup of tea, if you wave a small red ball in front of his face.

Well done. I love you boy!

BASIL MAKING MUMMY PROUD AT PUPPY CLASS

Chapter 9: THE TROUBLE WITH TALKING

Being out with a dog can sometimes turn you into public property, it's very similar to how an obviously pregnant woman feels. Everyone either looks at you, has a comment to make, makes a noise, wants to touch or engage you in some kind of conversation. It can range from the sublime *"your dog just made me smile"* to the ridiculous *"if I had your dog I would call it Gucci"*.

I remember once a very small Basil and I were standing alone in the big Homebase car-park just off the Finchley Road, a smart looking man passed by and nodded and waved, indicating that he too was probably a dog lover and wanted to acknowledge the tiny pup, a calm encounter of mutual understanding. I was holding Basil in my arms as he was still too small to be put on the ground and hadn't had his jabs yet. But I thought he might appreciate some fresh air so we kept standing under a tree breathing in the summer, he wrinkled his nose appreciatively and we cuddled happily. I was enjoying the quiet and warm feel of Basil's still velvety fur against my cheek when our peace was suddenly shattered by the sound of two women shrieking. Turning round I saw two middle-aged ladies running out of the large store, scarves flying out behind them, their heels clattering on the tarmac and they were heading straight for us.

"*That man, that man*" they squealed "*he said you had a freshly baked pup out here*". It was an ambush. That smart man had gone into Homebase and obviously couldn't help himself from expressing what he had just seen in the car park to two complete strangers! We were surrounded. There was nothing for it but to play along and Basil was kissed and cooed over for a long while as I waited desperately for Patrick to hurry up buying his plywood. I'm not good at making small talk with strangers but having a dog has meant I've had to have an upgrade in my social skills for sure. Maybe they should have included a session for us owners at Puppy Class?

But the fact that a lot of people want to comment on your dog or talk to you about it can lead you down a sinister path... Many want to talk about their own deceased dogs, so be warned! They suck you in with an innocent comment about your dog or dogs in general and then hit you with it: "*Yes our Sandy died last year, hit by a car*" or "*Maggie, she lasted until she was 10, but we couldn't let her suffer anymore. Cancer*". They fix you with a moist gaze and with a wobbly voice go on to describe the worst aspects of an illness, how they died and how the family felt afterwards. Some even start reaching for tatty photos still carried in wallets. It's terrible. It can come from any quarter and usually while you are a trapped, captive audience: cab drivers, people in lifts, guys working in shops - the bereaved dog owner can appear anywhere.

While I feel their pain I just hate it. I find myself flinching as soon as someone opens a dog conversation with me just waiting for that killer line. I know it's because I dread the day it's me telling the same tale to a hopeful new young owner with a tear in my eye.

Owning the same breed of dog allows you to open up a conversation with just about anyone. A wary dog-owner will tolerate your comments and attention, but if you open up with *'we've got a Boxer at home too, a boy Basil'* they will actually look at you, smile and gladly chat away about all things Boxer - which usually involves discussing how good they are with kids, how bouncy they are and how they act like puppies for most of their lives. You're in the special 'My Breed Too' club and worthy of a conversation. You're also allowed to give their dog a good stroke, a cuddle and a kiss and remark on the size of their chops without reproach. I will always approach a Boxer owner in the street and give my time to other owners who approach me. I know this is the same for all other breeds.

We talk to Basil all of the time. But not with any kind of purpose. If we're alone in the house together I will chat away to him, ask him his thoughts on a particular outfit or song. We soon forgot the one-word commands he was meant to learn and ended up just talking to him as if he was human. To this day he still only really understands the following

English: *"Where's Mummy?", "Where's Daddy?"* and *"Walkies to the park with a ball".*

We definitely have a tendency to anthropomorphise Basil, often attributing him with outlandish personalities and corresponding phrases and accents, rather like Johnny Morris used to do. Our favourite persona for him is a kind of flamboyant Quentin Crisp type character, complete with withering one-liners and a very correct English accent. You certainly don't want to get on the wrong side of Basil!

And worryingly, as time has gone on, Patrick and I now use Basil to talk to each other, both pretending to be the dog (complete with arch voice) to try and persuade the other to get something from the kitchen or turn the TV over. *"Mummy says will you bring her wine in please Daddy, while you're up".*

Chapter 10: THE TROUBLE WITH WALKING

As soon as Basil had had his final jabs and we could start walking him properly outside I believed that life would get immediately easier. It meant we could start going out again, we weren't chained to the car, he could go to the loo outside and of course we would have a gorgeous attention-grabbing pup to parade around Soho.

Poor Basil just didn't take to it straight away; despite his socialisation classes he found everything and everyone bewildering. The streets of Soho and Camden, where he took his first faltering steps outside, aren't known for being calm and reassuring and I did feel sorry for him as each car, bike, wheelchair or group of screaming hen-do goers seemed to roar past him. Every couple of steps he would resolutely sit down and look up at us as if to say *'Carry Me Daddy'* – he couldn't understand why he had to now make his own way on his own four feet.

Retrospectively I feel terrible that I used to get so exasperated with him for being so nervous. Thinking about it - the things he saw and had to go through would put off even the most eager human tourist in central London.

It was Soho in Summer and everyone had taken to the streets, it's great fun and I love the fact that Old Compton Street suddenly fills up with every type of character you can think of as soon as the sun comes out. But it's not so fun when you have a tiny, vulnerable pup to take care of. The kind of life that I found exciting and interesting was totally petrifying to the young, uninitiated Basil.

The world was full of loud drag queens, groups of huddled pimps and dealers, confused tourists, myriad-legged stag dos, happy revellers and plenty of drunken dropouts, all of whom would take an interest in him. It was mainly comments, ranging from the dramatic *'I'm just going to stand over here and quietly cry over your pup'* and *'Oh My God will you look at that little angel'* to the rather more worrying: '*can I walk your dog?*', '*why won't you let us touch your dog*' and '*I'm going to have that dog*'.

But the reaction was mainly positive and I found my life suddenly punctuated with squeals of delight as we walked the streets (it took me a while to realise that it wasn't me attracting the admiring glances). Many times I had to pause as Basil had his picture taken on yet another camera phone. Who knows where all the pictures in the world of Basil are but it makes me laugh to think of the amount of tourists who got home to find that their holiday snaps include a shot of a tiny Boxer puppy whose name they don't even know.

For me there was a bit of a downside to all this attention, as soon as we took to the streets I found that suddenly everybody wanted to touch him. Now, I am not normally squeamish but I worried that he could get contaminated by the slightest thing and when you have such a young, gorgeous looking pup everyone feels that they can just reach out and physically interact with him in some way.

I CAN SEE WHY HE WAS POPULAR

Poor Bas would constantly find hands thrust into his mouth or onto his head, it was so much for one so young. I became obsessed with keeping him clean and took to carrying him around again through the busiest streets and wouldn't make eye contact with eager, would-be dog polluters who seemed to approach from every street corner and mucky doorway.

I found that most people didn't even register me, just him. That is still true to this day. He always gets a lot of attention. I remember one occasion when I felt particularly left out: walking through Soho a big group of European tourists descended upon us and literally, without even acknowledging me, grabbed the young Basil and swung him up for a cuddle and a photo. One man in particular took a delight in him and while all of them were chatting to each other about Boxer dogs they had known, this ringleader made many jokes to his gang about stealing him! There was not one word to me apart from to ask his name, and as one of them was actually from Basle, it caused more hearty gales of laughter and more entreaties between themselves to have him away. Eventually they put him down and went on their way casting many looks back at the confused Basil.

Or there was the time we nearly caused a car crash. On crossing the road near our home we heard the squealing of brakes and honking of car horns. Turning we saw a man jumping out of a white van that had screeched to a halt next to us right in the middle of the traffic flow. He just had to leap out to let us know that he had a Boxer dog at home in his native Italy and they really were the best dogs. While we were pleased to hear it we weren't sure it was worth nearly getting into a crash for and after a little cuddle with Basil he ended up having an argument with the drivers of the two cars that had nearly driven into him as we walked on.

Soon the faltering, little pup grew up and gained a bit of strength, which meant walks took on a whole new meaning. Patrick never has trouble with Basil pulling, but sometimes I do. It's not that he pulls me so much as he is usually quite eager to get to where he is going. I totter along behind him wailing *'but you don't even know where we are going'* - which isn't strictly true if we are taking our well-worn path to the park. Basil gets so frantic to get there even quicker that his little paws turn into crampons and literally claw their way along the road. I sometimes think he gets worried that the park might disappear before we get there.

Regents Park, North West London was our local park, and how lucky we were to have it so close to us and for it to be the place where Basil learnt about the world. This famous, beautiful, central city space was where Basil really defined himself as a dog. He adored the place, he would know when he was anywhere near it and nearly kill himself trying to get there. We learnt a lot about our dog and the canine world from spending so much time there, such as:

- Basil loves a ball. In fact he loves a ball so much a walk without one is almost wasted. He will run and run after one, he will throw his leg out with cramp and still run and run after one. Footballs are best. We had to steer clear of the regular football games that take place in the park as Basil would happily sail off into the middle of play and claim the ball for his own to the cries of *'Get that bloody dog off the pitch'* and causing us much embarrassment. Every ball that comes into our house belongs to Basil, no question, the same goes for balloons.

- Dog owners fall into various groups, usually defined by your age or chosen breed. Rarely do we speak to groups outside of our accepted allies. Poodle owners will never speak to Bulldog owners as a blunt example. Older owners of larger hounds and gun dogs are the hardest group to crack. One suspicious chap in a flat cap and with a fine pair of Weimaraners came up behind us to inspect Basil's nether regions once, and on muttering *'good, good he's been done'* allowed his hounds to walk near us. The cheek! Patrick got into trouble once for declaring loudly near a Weimaraner owner that these gorgeous silver hounds were merely *'show off dogs'*, she rounded on him spitting *'how dare you, my dog is a working dog thank you very much'*. Which told him.

- Basil has a real sense of his own place in the animal world's pecking order. On walking past London Zoo he would go crazy for the smells of the nearby goats and sheep and try to bark through the wire at them. But the second we'd hear the roar of a lion or the honk of a llama he would immediately, submissively fall to the floor. (It was the same on a country walk through some open land populated by a few massive cows, our usually bullish dog turned decidedly sheepish when he saw the huge animals. If a dog could tip-toe he was doing it).

• A dog's sense of smell really is sensational. Basil can sniff out a muddy puddle a mile off, he will lose all sense of ownership and hare off into the distance in order just to take roll in the gorgeous stuff. He's usually rock hard by the time we get home, his bottom half completely set stiff in mud.

• Dogs have emotions. I am not sure how anyone who has seen one let loose to run free through the grass could disagree. It is the very definition of happiness.

We often say that when Basil passes away, no matter where we live in the country, Patrick will take his ashes to Regent's Park and leave them there with a football so he can carry on playing.

We were concerned about him pulling on the lead so much and possibly choking so we bought him a little head collar to replace the one that went around his neck. But this was swiftly replaced by a full body harness as walks were ruined by Basil spending more time trying to free the facial straps from round his squashed, snub nose – these things aren't made for Boxer dogs. The body harness is great fun, it looks like he is wearing a parachute from the front as the two black straps cross over on his white chest, and when he pulls forward his two front legs come up. Anyway he soon got used to it and now knows that when the harness comes out it's *'walkies'* time.

He doesn't yank me around so much anymore and thankfully he has only pulled me to the floor once, and that wasn't really Basil's fault as I was a bit tipsy on Chablis, talking on the mobile, wearing high heels and trying to hold his lead all at the same time! It wasn't just the dog learning lessons the hard way.

He can usually go without a lead for most of his walks now, unless we are near a main road, he'd never run away from us. He's quite single minded and if he has his own ball to play with then he'll not usually bother anyone else. But I'll never forget the time we were once walking across Primrose Hill, Basil was darting here, there and everywhere having a fine time. He had his small ball with him that day. We came across a family having a picnic; their children were playing with a football. Oh no! Football trumps small ball. Basil decided it was to be his and casting his little plaything to one side he made a beeline right for them. I started running after him shouting his name causing the family to look around startled at what was heading right towards them. But it was too late, a flying Basil was already committed to the air...

Of course he landed with a bump right in the middle of their picnic-rug sending the sandwiches and beakers of Pimms flying, before nosing off their football. It took an age to get hold of him so pleased was he with his new acquisition he'd decided to parade it around the whole of the hill for everyone to see. Eventually I managed to get hold of him, put him on the lead and with a grim face handed the deflated gooey ball back to the crying children. I apologised for the ruined food to the disgusted family and hurried him home. On turning a corner I started laughing and laughing as I remembered their horrified faces on seeing Basil flying through the air above them. I gave him a hug. Yes it was terrible behaviour but there is no point in crying over spilt Pimms right?

If you own a hound then walking is just a fact of life, you have to get used to it. Tired, hungover, no matter, you just need to get out there. Patrick always says that *'dogs need to pick up their messages'* – which just means sniffing other dogs wee, I've even heard of the term 'weemails' but I wouldn't use that myself. Now I have a lot of experience I can tell you twelve things that will definitely happen on a dog walk with Basil:

- Basil will chase after a discarded carrier bag in the road or something equally stupid that will make both of you look silly
- Basil will have a poo just as I have put the bags away or run out of them
- Basil will try to chase or catch someone else's ball despite having his own
- If I've had a big night out, look rough or haven't washed my hair I'll bump into someone I know, usually when Basil is having a poo
- Basil's fantastic football skills will prompt a passer-by to comment on the fact he is just what the England team needs right now
- Another dog will attempt to sniff or play with Basil, but will be ignored in favour of his ball
- You don't want to but can't help but look as the bum sniffing goes on
- Someone will attempt to catch Basil's attention by clucking or whistling, but will be ignored in favour of his ball
- A cheesewire will occur – this is where Basil walks behind you causing the lead to cut you

across the back of the legs – if not dealt with promptly it can bring you to the floor

- Someone will back away from us warily and act as if I've got a ferocious lion on the end of the lead, not a dog
- I'll say hello to the same dog walkers I see every day, I know their dogs name but not theirs
- If I've got a hangover it will be gone by the time I've finished a good circuit of the park (honestly a dog walk is the best cure and you usually pass a café selling coffee and bacon sandwiches too)

Chapter 11: THE PRESSING OF FLESH

Buoyed up by Basil's new found social skills and the fact we had been cooped up inside with him for so long we felt that a trip away was in order. We decided on Brighton as the place for Basil's grand unveiling to the public, we have always loved it, we have great friends who live there and the best hotel on the seafront – The Grand – allows dogs to stay! I imagine as a throwback to the days when wealthy socialite ladies used to carry round Pekes and Pugs during their annual jaunt to the coast?

Armed with numerous toys and treats (in fact his weekend away bag was bigger than mine) we headed off for the seaside. As this was to be Basil's first stay in a hotel he had a brush and a bath and his collar was cleaned, and after an exciting drive full of ocean smells we arrived at the hotel. The staff were (and still are) amazing and welcomed Basil as they would a treasured guest, although we knew it helped that he looked like the cutest puppy on earth. Sadly to mark the occasion Basil walked onto the reception carpet and promptly weed, I started to remonstrate loudly about his little indiscretion but Patrick with a furious, quietening look at me just pulled him smartly to the lift and no more was said or done. Sorry to everyone at The Grand Hotel.

A walk was in order, and after settling into our sumptuous room (complete with *'Caution: Dog in Room'* sign), the three of us set out onto the promenade. Nothing could have prepared us for the commotion he caused! As debuts go this one was a veritable sensation. Enlivened by the Summer sun and general holiday bonhomie in the air everyone was prepared to be 'wowed' by the gorgeous, tiny, silky puppy taking faltering steps along the seafront. We seemed to create a kind of avalanche of reactions, crowds started to gather and as people realised something was going on they started staring, making a beeline for us and shouting out to friends to come and look.

At one point we had a queue of people waiting to meet him, all eyes shining with tears or love or glee! It was amazing and totally took us by surprise. We listened to everyone's stories of how they had lost their own dog, or were desperate to get their own puppy or just those who wanted to express their joy at seeing him today. We magnanimously allowed gentle taps and strokes as we held him in our arms, we made sure the smaller kids at the back got through for a chance to say hi to him, we encouraged old folks not to be shy and come over as they hovered anxiously nearby. It was honestly like fielding a celebrity through the crowds, and gave us the same kind of kudos that day on the beach. (But I get it, I feel the same about puppies today, let me at them!)

As we bumped along the front we couldn't get more than two or three steps without another eager approach or a cheery wave and a shout of *'Gorgeous Puppy'*. It was also my first experience of *'Look, it's a little Charlie'*, this is something that happens still, owners of other Boxer dogs will see yours and give it their dog's name! It's a fun thing to do as it puts you all in that little 'My Breed Too' club and I always look at other slim, brindle Boxers now and say *'Look, he's like our Basil'*.

Eventually we had to get Basil back to the hotel – it was a lot for a small pup to take in and we didn't want to keep him out too long. We had to start turning people away, explaining he had had enough for one day, and hurried back to our sanctuary.

That evening we took Basil round to our friends' house for dinner and a lovely evening was had by all – a bit too lovely and we all got a bit drunk. So when we got back to the hotel I insisted we stay up and take Basil to the bar for another drink. Sadly the bar is one place they don't allow dogs, but after a bit of a discussion with staff a compromise was reached that allowed us to sit on the very edge of the bar with Basil lying on the reception carpet next to us. Having a dog wasn't going to stop me carrying on enjoying the evening!

Hungover the next morning we decided to go down for breakfast – if you have a hangover the breakfast at The Grand is not to be missed, and we had forgotten the night before to order breakfast in bed. Still tired from greeting his public the day before Basil continued to snooze in the warm, cosy room, so leaving him with a teddy and a treat we went downstairs to gratefully feast on a full English.

Making our way back upstairs a little bit later, fuller and happier, we heard an odd noise on coming out of the lift onto our floor. A kind of low, plaintive, stuttering note that flooded the spacious landing with rising and falling tones. It took us both a heartbeat to realise it was Basil – and he was howling! It was the first time we had heard it. We both literally flew round the corners and down the corridors to get to him – we actually broke into a run both feeling frantically for the room key shouting *'we're coming baby'* and *'mummy and daddy are here darling'* – I swear that corridor got longer and longer the nearer we got to the room so desperate were we to get to him.

Throwing open the door we fell upon the poor howling pup, obviously scared and lonely in the hotel room without us. We felt terrible! Even the fact we had smuggled up some delicious sausages from downstairs for him didn't make us feel any better –

even though he soon cheered up at the sight of them.

That dreadful sound is not one we hear often thankfully, but if me and my husband want to upset ourselves or each other now we replicate the howling young Basil as it still has the power today to make us feel sad and terrible.

The weekend continued happily despite that breakfast hiccup and Basil got to spend a little bit of time running on the beach and dabbling in the surf. His terror of being left alone in an unfamiliar hotel room was nearly usurped by his terror of moving water as he greeted the sea for the first time, but he soon got used to it.

Chapter 12: THE BRIGHT LIGHTS OF THE CITY

Working and going out in Soho with a good looking young dog gets you noticed and Basil soon started becoming a bit of a local figure, in fact he very soon took to his urbane lifestyle and became a proper town dog.

Every morning I would pop into the newsagent opposite my office for my daily 20 Silk Cut, and if Basil wasn't with me they always asked after him. We would then walk past my favourite local restaurant Balans, where I had (and still do) a very good relationship with the friendly, handsome staff. If my favourite waiter was standing outside having his morning cigarette we would always stop and chat and he usually had a sausage in his apron for Basil. If I was popping in for lunch (which I usually did) then he would let me know what meat was on the menu so they could put a couple of bones by for me to take home.

For obvious reasons Basil came to love this man and soon he began jumping up at anyone standing outside the restaurant because he knew this was where his sausage and bone supply was coming from. Sometimes it was just innocent diners popping out for a fag. It took a bit of time to explain what was going on and no they weren't expected to provide him with any meaty products. Actually Basil was happy to jump up and shake hands with anyone we stopped to chat with, I never had the heart to mention the Pee Paws – these were usually professionals working in the food industry!

I had to take him out for little walks in the day especially while training him in the art of going to the toilet outside. Opposite my office there was a well-tended garden which is actually a small churchyard. We often used to go in there for a run around with a ball and to wait for an age while Basil deliberated whether or not to have a wee or a poo. One beautiful morning he decided to go for a roll around in some newly planted flowers, before I could get to him the garden-keeper came flying out of his little shed and gave the bewildered Basil a good ticking off before giving me one too. His barely grown blooms were crushed and so were we.

This little city garden was also a regular walking ground for Soho's other canine residents, including the naughty pug who insisted on trying to debag Basil on sight (despite being a quarter of his size) and the two terriers who faithfully followed their flamboyant owner around with all three noses in the air, studiously ignoring us. Even their poo looked like little pearls.

We used to throw a little ball against the tomb of William Hazlitt, a long dead local writer and radical, until we were put off, not by the garden keeper this time but by the barking that was coming from across the road. It seemed that every time we indulged in a bit of ball play against the mausoleum another dog was aggrieved. I eventually managed to track the source and spied in a high up window surveying the whole of Soho a huge Boxer bitch looking intently in our direction and bellowing if I so much as took the ball out of my pocket. Maybe Hazlitt had a Boxer dog in his lifetime and here we had a living canine guardian protecting his grave today?

Sometimes in the evening the temptation of a few drinks and a bit of company was too strong to ignore. I didn't turn down every invitation and sometimes had to trail around Soho looking for a spot we could go with Basil. Central London isn't very accommodating when it comes to drinking and dining with dogs so we were always at a bit of a loss if it wasn't warm enough to sit outside. Naughtily sometimes we ignored the No-Dog rule and often stowed Basil under a table or a bar stool so he could slumber or eat a few crisps whilst hiding from the staff. But we were often chucked out. You could still smoke indoors in those days and he often came home smelling of fags, poor chap.

This was me still trying to fit my new dog into my old life and it probably wasn't the most responsible behaviour. But Basil always seemed unperturbed at being in a loud, busy pub or standing in a rainy street whilst trying to hail that elusive empty black cab (and one that takes dogs). This did become a bit of a problem trying to get home after a few drinks in Soho. If you think acting in a drunken manner will put off potential cab drivers then standing hopefully on the corner with a dog will certainly do so. I've been turned down so many times because I had Basil with me I took to hiding him behind my legs and shopping bags, only revealing him at the last minute as I'd bundle him up into the back of the car. Once a driver turned round to spot Basil being surreptitiously pushed into his taxi and he swore and shoo-ed us out. As he sped off leaving us by the side of road I shouted out *'you're lucky, normally I'd be throwing up in the back of your cab, not just leaving a few dog hairs behind'*. Terrible behaviour, the poor guy could have had an allergy!

The cab drivers that did stop for us were usually dog lovers themselves so we'd end up having chats about our pooches on the journey home. Sometimes Basil would get on the seat and look out of the window much to the amusement of cars we'd pull up next to at the lights.

But waiting for a cab is always more preferable than trying to take a dog on a late night drunken London bus and I just wouldn't do it. Not for my own safety – I've been mugged, propositioned, insulted, pushed over and asked for a fight on the No29 and I'd still happily hop on it if I saw one trundling down the road – but for Basil's. I probably wouldn't be able to protect him from a group of scary chaps intent on taking him off me.

We decided to compile a list of pubs that allowed dogs and stick to it. This resulted in a fabulous find just 15 minutes' walk from our home. This was a friendly pub full of other dog owners and amazing staff who swoop on their canine clients as soon as you arrive with offers of treats and water bowls. It can take longer for a human to be served. We spent many happy summer days sitting in the garden, drinking cava and watching Basil be petted by the bar staff.

Our local pub in Camden knows Basil really well! Because it was only three doors down from our home we would go there quite a lot so it was very easy for him to remember it. Often when we'd amble past on an innocent walk at any time of the day, he'd rush up to the door, jump up and look through the window, trying to get in. It's rather embarrassing behaviour really as you don't want everyone to assume you go to the pub so often that even the dog knows the way – even if it is true.

Chapter 13: THE COMING OF AGE

We know that Basil's birthday is May 23rd from his Kennel Club certificate. As his first birthday started getting closer I decided that he should have a party. I always have a party and it seemed unfair for him not to. From my trawling of the internet to find dog-related websites I knew there was a farm in the Midlands that specialised in making unusual dog foods. For a hefty fee they would be able to laser print a picture of your pooch in edible dye onto a birthday cake that could be eaten by humans and canines... seemed a great idea. They also provided other party comestibles such as fish flavoured ice-cream and dog biscuits that spelt out Happy Birthday. I decided to get ordering. The date was in the diary and I started issuing invitations to everyone who knew Basil and had a good response back.

On the day Basil had a bath and brush in anticipation. It was to be held in the office at lunchtime and so I decorated it with balloons and party food. The cake had safely arrived and looked amazing, the fish ice-cream was slightly smelly, there were presents wrapped up and more dog biscuits and treats laid out than Basil could eat in a week! I stopped the team working and made them come over to Basil's birthday celebration area, Patrick and a few local friends arrived (those that couldn't make it sent apologies, cards and presents) and a party was had. Of sorts. It's kind of hard to toast the birthday boy when he can't speak and doesn't know what's going on. Still he ran around a bit with his new ball, tried some cake and ice-cream, got thoroughly over excited and had his photo taken for the cake-farm's website – just like any kid at his first birthday party I suppose. Everyone stood around with forced smiles on their faces, patting the dog and gingerly trying the human/dog hybrid food.

Eventually people started drifting back to their desks or left and despite me trying to declare the whole thing a resounding success, a lovely guy who works in my office, summed it up best by sitting down and muttering: *'let's never speak of this again'.* I believe you can still find the photos online somewhere.

BASIL'S 1st BIRTHDAY CAKE! SERIOUSLY

Now for his birthday we usually make do with a new football, a steak and a couple of cards just between us in the family, although he does still receive a card from the office, even if having another party is just not mentioned.

A fun thing about having a dog is that for every single occasion you now get given dog-themed cards – birthdays, Christmas, Valentines etc – people always think they are the first to find that card for you with the picture of a girl in high-heels walking a dog. And Boxer dog faces do lend themselves well to cards that say disparaging things about age like '*A tad older...?*' or '*It's not so bad!*'

Patrick and I do send each other birthday and Christmas cards pretending to be from the dog – you can actually buy ones that say '*Happy Christmas from The Dog*'! They get more and more elaborate as the occasions go by, and for my last birthday poor Basil had his paws dipped in ink to press the print of them into my card.

But yes, Basil was growing up. Despite still acting like a puppy – and he has continued to do so his whole life, which is a definite Boxer trait – his fur had changed, it had grown from that unbelievably soft velvet into something a lot coarser. He also no longer had that lolloping puppy gait that makes one so easily identifiable from just a small fully grown dog.   When viewed from far away I always think puppies look like they are just a bit fuzzy around the edges.

And his bark had changed. This is the equivalent of a boy's voice dropping when he becomes a teen. After a few squeaks and starts his adorable yelp turned into a big dog bark. It's quite surprising when it happens and all three of us got a shock when this deep woof came out of his mouth, we all looked round in surprise to see who had done it! *Our boy is growing up'* remarked Patrick. I felt a bit miserable about it.

Now he could 'talk' properly Basil took to woofing as much as he could, he seemed to enjoy testing out his new found skill. Patrick or I would be sitting on the sofa and Basil would walk right up to us put his face as close as possible to ours and 'Woof' as loudly as he could. It was alarming and charming all at the same time. Thankfully this particular habit only lasted a few months and now he only woofs when someone comes to the door, which can be rather useful when you can't hear the doorbell.

He also started indulging in a bit of what we call 'gentleman's time' and licking his bits and bobs and being slightly more interested in what goes on down there. Like a real life teen. I hesitate to use the description 'lipstick' because I find it rather distasteful but you know what I am talking about? Sadly for Basil becoming sexually active was not to be in his future and we had him 'done'. He still likes a bit of 'gentleman's time' and without really knowing why he'll come and stand over your foot when you have your legs crossed and hover there trying to get a rub from a toe or two! Bless him, all those natural instincts never to be used.

Basil sadly had been docked as a tiny puppy, this practise is all but illegal now and I have to say that I would have loved for him to have a big, waggy tail. Poor Basil though, he has a tail that looks like a thick thumb hitching a lift, it twitches from side to side as fast as it can when he is happy. Sometimes it twitches just on hearing my voice, which I will always love him for. Because it is so small he has to wag his whole behind when he is especially excited.

When you come home he will be wagging his back end so hard he usually ends up going round in a circle. He'll also have a toy or sock in his mouth to welcome you through the door.

I do love approaching the house when Basil is indoors because he does the typical canine greeting of bouncing up and down as high as he can for you, ears flapping everywhere. As you are reaching around in your bag for your keys and looking through the glass you see: Dog. Nothing. Dog. Nothing. Dog. Nothing. Dog. Nothing. I sometimes stand outside longer than I need to because I enjoy the show so much.

So yes Basil was starting to do 'adult dog things' and he had grown up to be a gorgeous looking boy too – still eye-catching with his red and black stripes, he had also taken on the familiar Boxer mask like face with a distinctive white stripe down his nose. And of course, he's got four white adorable socks and a snow-white bib. He has an open, eager face that always looks like he is smiling and he lollops around good naturedly.

Sadly he has rubbish teeth though, right from when he was a pup, his mouth is full of missing molars and cracked canines. But thankfully, he has never grown those long extended drooling chops, so pertinent to the breed, or put on a huge amount of weight. In fact he has a rather dainty figure that is often commented upon. He is certainly the slimmest member of my household. Despite our previous misgivings he happily hasn't turned out like his short, fat mother or his large, lumbering father (that's his canine parents by the way, not his human ones!)

Chapter 14: THE MAKING OF MISTAKES

Probably the main mistake was getting a dog in the first place because we sometimes felt so ill-equipped to deal with him. (I often wonder what happens to those people who buy tiny, fashionable dogs to keep in their handbags then realise they are responsible for a life?)

But yes like most people I make mistakes, many of them related to dog ownership. I have made the following errors and wouldn't recommend them to any dog owner:

- After a walk in the local dog toilet – my friend's rather charming name for the little patches of ring-fenced land you find in London laid on for a dog's convenience – Basil's paws were obviously covered in other dogs poop. For some reason I can't explain I thought spraying him with bleach would be a good idea. As I set about him with the toxic spray Patrick came running in crying *'you can't do that he's a living creature'* I'm really not sure what I was thinking.

- During a raucous gathering of drunken ladies round mine that we laughably called 'Book Club' Basil managed to escape. An attendee had left our gate open and on letting her in he had seen his way free into the open main road outside our house. It was the first time he had done it and was still very small. I hared off after him and screamed and screamed as I dodged cars in my bare feet. His imminent death would certainly be my fault. I didn't calm down all evening, even after he was safely indoors and had panic dreams for a few nights after.

- I've let him eat grapes and chocolate – both of which are toxic to dogs – after carelessly exclaiming *'a little bit won't do him any harm'*, which is terribly dangerous because you never know how your dog will react. Thankfully Basil has always been a good at vomiting and if he ever does eat anything that disagrees with him you'll find it in a wet pile on the floor only minutes later.

- I've lost count of the times I've put the spoon in my mouth after serving up a tin of dog food. It's automatic isn't it? Finish dishing up something tasty you suck on the spoon. Except it isn't tasty. In fact it doesn't taste of anything. It is more of a 'feeling'. Gelatinous. If you've never had dog food in your mouth trust me on this one.

- I once had to get hold of Basil for some reason when he was running away from me. I rushed up behind him and grabbed his back-end as he squirmed around, but as my fingers closed around him one of my thumbs kept on going... I had pressed it right into his bum! He whipped round to look at me. We locked eyes for a split second, both of us absolutely appalled, before I plucked out my offending digit with a sob and ran off to wash my hands.

We circled each other warily for a few hours after that, neither sure how to approach the other ever again.

Bad times.

Chapter 15: THE KINGDOM OF BED

As I have said before this is not a training book and nothing you read here should be taken as a recommendation for your own dog if you have one - especially this bit about the BED! Every trainer or training book will tell you not to allow your dog to sleep with you, it's something to do with the dog feeling equal or superior to you. I really tried to subscribe to this as I felt strongly about keeping Basil in his place and having the marital bed as sacred to me and Patrick. However, despite my best efforts, all three of us sleep together now in one big pile - like packs of dogs in the wild.

Here's how this came about and the problems associated with letting your dog sleep on your bed. After Basil had got used to us and the house a bit more we tried to leave him downstairs at night with the light off and the door shut, it seems harsh but he had his favourite chair to sleep on and access to his outside space. Despite looking at us miserably as we closed the door and scampered up to our clean bed, it didn't really seem to worry him and he was usually quiet throughout the night. However, as soon as dawn broke and any light started filtering through to his room the barking would start – little questioning woofs at first but building up to full blown roaring. Now, there is an argument that if you have a dog you should always be up and ready for the walking and feeding and watering, however, when the dog in question is woofing from first light in summer around 5am then the argument is flawed.

In order to stop the dawn chorus coming from downstairs (and in all probability annoying the neighbours) one of us would have to get up and let him out of his room. The little devil was always ready to shoot up the stairs and jump straight onto the bed – after a quick cuddle he would promptly fall straight back to sleep and get quite indignant when we had to re-emerge bleary eyed to get ready for work just a few hours later. Yes, thanks for that boy.

The morning cuddles became quite a tradition and eventually Basil was so at home on the bed that some evenings he would be allowed to spend all night on the bed *'as a treat'* thanks to Daddy – it was usually a night when Mummy was a bit tipsy and therefore too weak to put up a fight and only allowed on the presumption that we would put him back downstairs the next night. After a few *'treat'* nights in a row it was eventually considered *'cruel'* to put him back downstairs and after a discussion I discovered that *'Basil sleeps up here now doesn't he?'* So there we go, the three of us now sleep together on the bed. It helps that we have a large bed but now that Basil has grown considerably from when he was a pup you can't hide the fact that it is like having a third person curled up with you - usually around knee height – meaning my husband and I have had to develop some unusual sleeping shapes in order to accommodate him.

He creates a kind of black hole in the middle of the bed that all duvets and bedspreads get sucked into, he honestly has his own linen orbit. For some reason he weighs a lot more at night than during the day. We are forever pulling the duvet round ourselves trying to avoid waking up in the night with half our body exposed to the cold while Basil burrows into his cosy nest between us.

And he really fights for that position on the bed. As soon as we start making moves to retire for the evening you can guarantee that if Basil isn't already up there (he often takes himself off to bed early to get a good spot) he'll be up the stairs before you've locked the front door and turned the lights off. And as he has got older and bolder he has started staging a coup for the prime pillow spot – it's not enough that he sleeps on the bed he likes to have his head on a pillow too. Woe betide the last one in bed because you'll find both top positions gone.

Once when I was particularly slow in getting ready, I came into the bedroom to find Patrick reading on his side of the bed and Basil on mine with the duvet pulled up around him and eyeing me warily. I pretended to get into the bottom of the bed to make my point that we were both in the wrong place, hoping that he might realise that he should be down there, not me, and move. He merely lifted his head up from the pillow, looked at me witheringly for a couple of seconds, before snuggling back down, shutting his eyes and seeming to fall asleep immediately. I felt so reduced I almost did sleep at the bottom of the bed that night.

The getting ready for bed routine can be touching though – the time Basil was a bit late in getting off the sofa and following us up to bed had us running round in glee getting the bed exactly as we liked it before he arrived. We felt terrible when we turned round to see him eagerly making his way towards the bedroom with his favourite toy bear in his mouth as if to say *'sorry I'm late I was just getting my teddy'*.

He also likes to turn endless circles before he settles down, going round and round and getting in the way of the TV or treading on your feet until he has got himself completely ready to plump down in the exact, correct position. Patrick says that this behaviour comes from wolves having to tread down the reeds in the wild to create a comfortable, circular clearing in which to sleep. I don't mind Basil displaying natural instincts but my sheets have a high thread count and are nothing like reeds.

I have to be honest here – it does play havoc with your love life. You just don't have the spontaneity of turning a gorgeous morning cuddle into something more when you have a dog lying between you. And he is usually snoring and farting. Yes, it's true, out of the three of us the dog definitely snores the loudest and his farts are absolutely terrible, as he grows older they get louder and smellier.

Quick aside here about farts: we used to find the fact our tiny puppy did them hilarious! They made cute noises and were virtually odourless. Now our big tripe eating hound makes loud embarrassing cracks that force us to push him off the sofa while holding our breath. Sometimes they are so strong they actually hurt to inhale. We call them *'aerosol shits'* because it can honestly smell like a muck spreader has sprayed some hideous turds into the room. You can cope when you are at home, but when you are in the pub or in the office it's not so good. People are affronted that you have allowed your dog to assault their nostrils so badly. We usually greet each emission with a curt *'Dirty Dog'* it's a satisfying phrase to say and makes sure anyone near you knows where the blame lies (and of course is a useful foil for any human stinkers!)

Anyway, back to bed… so yes, we find it hard to be as intimate as often as we would like thanks to the third member of our household making the bed his own. However, Basil seems unperturbed when we do. There has often been an occasion when thinking he was downstairs we have been getting frisky only to look round in the heat of the moment to find him staring at us questioningly, head cocked to one side, with a toy in his mouth as if to say *what ARE you doing?*' A few times he has leapt up on the bed halfway through much to our surprise and once we were so carried away we just put the duvet over him and carried on as he settled down to sleep through it.

There are other downsides to letting the dog sleep in the bed. My main problem is Dog Dust. This is what we call the film of grit that seems to accumulate after only a couple of days. It is made up of mud, dog hair and general dirt, you can't really see it but you can feel it when you run your hand over the sheets, like invisible sand, and it drives me mad. The calm sanctuary of the bedroom is a thing of the past for us as I am always furiously rubbing down the sheets before I get into bed complaining and muttering about how *'the bloody dog shouldn't be allowed up here anyway'* and *'now I am going to have to change the sheets again'*. I know everyone says it but honestly for me sometimes there is no greater pleasure than being the first to get into a newly changed bed.

Sharing your bed with a dog is so hard on your sheets, Egyptian cotton gets snagged and expensive bedspreads always end up looking mucky, and he always licks everything. Gone are the days when the bed can look fresh and white – I now favour darker coloured bed linen as I just can't bear to look at another paw print in the middle of a new white duvet cover and really, I would rather not know what all of the mysterious smudges are. We often laugh that if we were all murdered in our bed the forensic team would have a field day.

Instead of a temple to sleep and relaxation the bed has become a kind of dog playground. I've lost count of the amount of times I have slipped thankfully between the sheets only to find I am nestled up against a particularly ripe piece of cowhide or a saliva covered chew toy.

And if I decide he has to get off the bed – say if I have just changed the sheets and want to keep them free of the dreaded Dog Dust for at least until we all get into bed – he won't let me get anywhere near him. He'll spin round and round rucking up the sheets or hide under the covers. (Once while I was changing the sheets I left the mattress exposed for the day and Basil chewed all of the buttons off of it). Yes, I would say the bed is most definitely his.

But I would just say that, despite everything, I love seeing him stretch out in absolute bliss on the bed, he really extends to his full length in total joy. We call him the Longest Dog in The World. Sometimes he sleeps between us like a third person, and he is so happy and relaxed that we can all go to sleep with his head on the pillow next to ours and wake up eight hours later to find that he hasn't moved an inch all night.

And he can be so funny asleep – when he is in a deep, deep slumber his eyes slightly open but roll back into his head so we only see the redness, we call it Zombie Dog (*"walkies, sit, brains"*) and he starts dreaming. We always know when he is dreaming as he starts 'wiffling' which is a kind of soft yelping bark - or talking in your sleep for dogs - accompanied by a twitching leg. We know his fantasy of running with a football before a dinner of sardines is running film-like through his sleepy head. Sometimes he gets so carried away with his 'wiffling' that he starts shaking madly, juddering from side to side and waking everyone up, while he carries on sleeping regardless.

I'd never wake him up when he looks so comfortable but he doesn't think twice about getting everyone else up if he is keen to get on with the day. Patrick is never allowed a lie in at the weekend because Basil will just nose him and nose him until he gets up and takes him out, he knows that when Daddy is not getting ready for work it's a walkies with a ball day. And I am often woken up by a snorting, sniffling face pressed up against my own as Basil has come round to my side of the bed to burrow me out. It's quite disconcerting to open your eyes from sleep to find another big brown pair staring straight back at you first thing. I'm sure he finds it funny?

As much as I complain, we love having him so close to us. We all sleep better together. And when my husband is away for the night because of work I am thankful for Basil's keen ears and the familiar, warm weight of him - he'll usually take Patrick's pillow so I never really feel alone. And cuddling your dog in the morning before you go to work is wonderful – we have at least half an hour in bed every morning with a cup of tea to chat about the day and cuddle Basil. I think I like those parts of the day the best.

Chapter 16: THE DOING UP OF THE DOGHOUSE

Patrick and I loved our joint Camden flat but it was very much set up for a young working couple with expensive furnishings and a light colour scheme. We soon realised we were going to have to make our home more 'dog friendly'. While he was young and being house-trained there were plenty of accidents on the floor, in a room with floorboards this was ok, but in the rooms with carpets not so ok. We invested in various spray potions that promised to diminish every stain and smell and jet-powered water carpet cleaners that made loud noises, but we still ended up with carpets of a slightly different colour from the ones we had when we moved in.

Basil started to favour one room in particular for throwing up, if he needed to be sick he would always stagger to this room to do it. It became known as Basil's Vomitarium. Eventually we started pulling the carpets up as we just couldn't go on cleaning them – the whole flat ended up as floor boards, which then really collected the dog hair. You really can't win.

We also had to pull the carpets up for slightly more squalid reasons. Basil started to worry the edges of them to find loose strings to pull at and soon whole rows were disappearing. We didn't think about where they were disappearing to until one day Patrick was taking Basil for a walk, he noticed that the dog was trying to poo but having trouble and dragging his back end along the floor.

Leaning down to inspect Patrick saw a small brush like end poking out of Basil's backside – taking a deep breath he grabbed it and started pulling. And pulling, and pulling. He was drawing the carpet strings out from Basil's bum! Like a magician pulling endless handkerchiefs from his sleeve - only rather more unsavoury. We had to perform this trick quite a few times until we'd unravelled what remained of the rush-matting from his insides. Ta-da!

But it wasn't just the floors that had to be attended to, of course Patrick installed the little dog flap in the back door so Basil could get into the garden whenever he pleased but then had to spend hours constructing two little sets of steps so he could actually climb up to use it. The back garden had to be fortified with new gates and fencing and a myriad of other home improvements and precautions were made. Including moving the toilet roll holder up a foot higher so that Basil couldn't keep ripping the loo roll off and festooning the upstairs landing with his own paper bunting.

Around the time of getting Basil we also bought a brand new brown leather sofa from Camden Market – a very expensive but sumptuous corner unit that I loved. Some may say the timing was always going to be bad, but I thought because it was good leather it would be wipe clean and we could easily remove hairs from it. I didn't however, think that because it smelt so good and slightly animalistic it would be so attractive to Basil. Stray threads would be worried and worried until tiny holes began opening up along seams, soon huge holes started appearing and one day we came home to the innards of our lovely sofa strewn all over the floor.

We kept trying to patch it up using all manner of different tapes and leather samples, we even sent it back to Europe (where it was made) to be recovered – spending six weeks without a sofa, all of us sitting on the floor. But it just happened again and again. Eventually it became just a leather fringed frame sporting two huge holes stuffed with tea towels and covered over with big black plastic sheets, and only once it was totally ruined did Basil leave it alone, (*"my work here mummy is done!"*). My dog and I fell out terribly over that sofa.

BASIL'S FINEST WORK – THE SOFA

Chapter 17: THE FOLLOWING OF FASHION

It isn't just the home that has been modified, having a dog has definitely affected my wardrobe. Don't worry I didn't start suddenly buying jumpers with paw prints on them or anything (I know they are available however). But I found I had to take having a dog into account very quickly when it came to getting dressed in the morning. The usual staple of any girls' wardrobe – black – became a problem thanks to dog hair. It gets everywhere! Believe me once the dog hairs get in your black wash your clothes are doomed. I found myself sitting in meetings obsessed with pulling the little white hairs off of lovely new, black suits.

I remember once taking a dress out of the dry-cleaners in the morning, taking it straight to work and wearing it to a premiere that night and still finding some dog-hairs on it – it hadn't even been anywhere near the dog? There are now lint-rollers stashed everywhere – drawers at work, all handbags, coat pockets, in the car and in the bedroom.

But dog hairs getting everywhere isn't really Basil's fault, his obsession with shoes and socks however, I am sure can be helped. The young Basil took a delight in finding shoes and chewing them – usually beautiful, new high-heels – probably because the stiletto offers him something decent to get his teeth into? I can't discuss the shoes I have had to throw away here because I would cry. But it's terribly upsetting to have an outfit in mind and know the shoes that will go perfectly with it only to find that Basil has got there first and they are now adorned with teeth marks and ripped leather, meaning you have to hastily put together a whole new outfit.

Socks are a real problem. For some reason Basil doesn't like anyone to wear them. If he sees you putting them on he will try and help you to take them off. I am sure he thinks he is saving you from the evil things. Socks without holes are a precious commodity in our house.

I often find objects you just wouldn't think of as taking a dog's interest covered in bite marks or dried saliva: hair grips, hair brushes, laptop bags, make-up... Thankfully as he grew he needed to chew things less and less but I am still nervous about new shoes and hide them away.

I used to love slathering on creamy body lotions after a bath and expensive face creams as I got into bed, but when you share that bed with a pooch those unctions just attract Dog Dust and hair, so you wake up feeling like you've rolled in sand and have grown a beard overnight. And for some reason he always, always manages to step on my toes just after I've had a pedicure, smudging the fresh nail-polish. It's like he knows.

Having a dog and a dainty little handbag just doesn't go. You have so much stuff to take around with you and there aren't designer dog utility bags like there are for babies. (I really wish Cath Kidston would make a pretty dog tote in the same fabrics as her baby-changing bags). I needed larger and larger handbags to accommodate all of Basil's things.

Here are seven things that are now often to be found in my handbag:

- Poobags (when I remember obviously)
- Chewed piece of hide
- Tripe sticks
- Food pouches
- Tennis Ball
- Lint Roller
- Tin of Sardines in Oil

(Note: Lack of vomit, spare undies and an ashtray)

It's more embarrassing to pull a smelly piece of cow-hide out of your bag by mistake than a tampon girls, let me tell you! If only because it's harder to explain.

So I had to start shopping for clothes that didn't show up the dog hair for me, but I also started looking for things for Basil. Shopping is always wonderful even if it's not for yourself and there is a huge array of stuff out there you can buy a dog. I revelled in all the online shops and boutiques, and the trips to the massive pet supermarkets. I started taking as much interest in types of dog food as I would in a restaurant's exciting new menu.

But without a doubt the best and funniest of things you can buy are outfits. I was worried for a while that only the cute handbag type dogs would be catered for, but oh no - even Basil sized pooches get the pick of a wardrobe. And soon I realised even more potential in Basil to be a street-stopping accessory! His puppy-cuteness grabbed enough attention as it was - but add a studded-leather collar and a green hoodie that sported the word 'PUP' instead of 'GAP' and his appeal shot into the stratosphere.

The fact that Patrick and Basil hated all of it meant nothing to me and I ploughed on with endless outfits despite all of them eventually being confined to the bin. Here are some of the best (now lost) outfits that I still mourn to this day:

- **The Black Parka**: worn once but when we realised his style of weeing resulted in the furry white armbands being sprayed and turning yellow it went in the bin
- **The England Hoodie**: bought to support England in the 2006 World Cup, it lasted about as long as they did

- **The Santa Outfit**: to be worn in the lead up to Christmas to the delight of all seasonal revellers (the photo opportunities are endless) and my Nan who enjoyed Basil's delivery of a festive bottle of brandy dressed up in it
- **The Devil Outfit** – complete with horns: worn at a Halloween party where his photo was taken and sent in to Most Haunted Live! He looked totally miffed
- **The Dracula Outfit**: his second outfit for the Halloween party, pictures of him in it were used as invite for aforesaid party
- **The Red Reindeer T-shirt**: bought for Basil's second Christmas, a slightly more grown up tight t-shirt with googly eyes, he looked rather camp in it

Some outfits didn't have to be specifically for dogs – Patrick bought me a Tokyo t-shirt while on a business trip to Japan. He also bought the same design in a kids size for Basil and one of our best photos is a snap of both of us wearing our cool matching Japanese tees.

But I didn't only want Basil to dress up, I wanted him to scrub up too. I love a spa day myself. He's a short haired breed and needs very little grooming but I insisted that he should take a trip to the local pet parlour, despite Patrick insisting there no need. So just because I wanted to experience every aspect of owning a dog (I have a terrible problem with missing out on anything) poor old Basil was booked into a Primrose Hill salon for a shampoo, set, blow-dry and nail clip.

"You're going to love it pal" I whispered in his ear as he was signed into the holding pen, *"mummy does."* Patrick and I sauntered off for lunch leaving Basil behind to enjoy his pampering session. Returning an hour later slightly inebriated and full of the joys of Spring we picked up our rejuvenated pooch. He ran out to greet us, jumping into my arms and putting his head into my neck, obviously relieved to see us again. He felt super soft and silky and smelt beautifully of yellow flowers. I was delighted.

"How did he get on?" we asked.

"He hated it," was the answer.

He's never been back since.

TOKYO TWINS?

Chapter 18: THE CONSUMING OF PRODUCTS

But it wasn't just the clothes, dogs need lots of stuff and there is a whole commercial industry set up around them. Patrick and I threw ourselves in wholeheartedly! We delighted in buying him big plush toys - and still do - because he absolutely adores them. Every time we go away we bring him back something stuffed that represents where we have been, i.e a duck and bear from the US, a camel from Dubai and a fish from the Maldives. Toys for dogs are amazing these days, there is every type and shape you can think of, but for some reason every single one of them has to have a squeak! It's unbelievable that you can find a toy in the shape of a platypus if you so choose, but you can't find one that doesn't sound like a screeching pig when you touch it.

But if you do give Basil a soft toy sometimes his natural instinct will take over and he'll run around with it in his mouth shaking his head violently from side to side – before pinning the poor creature to the floor and opening it up, looking up at us gleefully as if to say *'look I killed it'*. We used to find this amusing until one day we noticed he was suffering from constipation, eventually he started passing what looked like stained, rough cotton wool – and he wasn't finding it easy. The poor lad was actually shitting kapok! We try not to let him open up soft toys anymore.

Despite a few shopping successes – such as the bronze double-bowl feeder in the shape of a standing Daschund bought from an antique shop in Suffolk – nearly everything I bought turned out to be a totally naff or useless purchase. I used to just put the words 'Boxer Dog' into eBay and see what would turn up before scouring online pet shops for something I could buy him. Madness.

Here are just some of my purchases and what happened to them:

- Big brown leather dog bed to match the sofa and nearly as expensive. He never used it despite me demonstrating it personally many times by pretending to go to sleep in it. Like the sofa it was sadly eaten.

- Soft dog blanket covered in Boxer dogs and bearing the legend: *My Blanket.* Also eaten.

- Rubber backed mat for the back door, covered in paw prints, to minimise real life paw prints muddying the floor. Not just eaten but pooed on beforehand.

- An A4 colour print of pop-art Boxer dog faces. Put in a drawer and never looked at again.

- A ball with a recordable soundchip – the idea is you record yourself saying reassuring phrases to your dog so that when he is left alone he can play with it and hear your voice. It also dispensed edible treats. Incredibly expensive but oddly ineffective and it certainly never sounded like me! The mechanism got gummed up with peanut butter.

- A pair of white dog towels embroidered with a Boxer face and the word BASIL. We put them proudly on display in our bathroom, but unbeknownst to us a friend secretly took a photo of them and revelled in showing it to our friends as an example of just how sad we had become. Now hidden away, we use them for scrubbing him down after muddy walks.

Over the years I haven't had much time to watch TV or keep up with the soaps because I was always out so often in the evenings. But spending more time at home and having a dog has opened up a whole new world of soap operas and Dog TV to me. There are absolutely loads of canine programmes and we are aficionados of all of them.

They fall into a few main categories:

- Naughty dogs need to get trained – usually the fault of the owner
- Fat dogs need to get slim because their health is at risk – always the fault of the owner
- Fat dogs and their owners both need to get slim and end up competing at an event
- Exposés of those who work in the dog world – usually includes heart-warming stories of RSPCA officers overcoming adversity or bad owners getting arrested (the American shows are better at this)

- Dogs doing jobs and performing amazing feats or heroic acts
- Rescue dogs overcoming difficulties and re-entering society thanks to charities or training centres
- Rescue dogs being trained up for special purposes such as being guide dogs or hearing dogs
- All of the above but featuring celebrities

Sometimes the odd Boxer dog will appear on one of these shows resulting in squeals of delight in our house and us shouting at the TV *'we'll have him'*.

The granddaddy of all of these shows has to be Crufts, usually broadcast from Birmingham once a year, and we love it. Three days of endless dogs prancing and posing on TV, punctuated by live links discussing the merits of one pooch above another. It's unadulterated doggy joy, we get so involved we cancel all social engagements, mark it in our diaries and end up watching the extra digital coverage late into the night.

This obsession with doggy-vision extends into films too. Due to the nature of our jobs my husband and I have a large film collection, and we have now created our very own dog-related section. I just have to seek out and watch any decent movie with a dog in it. I also read a huge amount of dog magazines and books (dogs helping others overcome disabilities, dogs changing people's lives, disadvantaged dogs being rehabilitated, funny dog tales, dog memoirs, misery tales about dogs dying etc) and I usually get a few canine books or films for Christmas from friends and family. We could open a shop.

I remember once I was reading probably the most famous dog memoir out there (the one made into a disappointing Hollywood film a few years back) I knew that the big golden Labrador died in the end but this didn't put me off and I set about enjoying the story. But of course, I became emotionally involved and really started to love that hound. Patrick found me sobbing in the bathroom one day, absolutely inconsolable, the book was open at my feet.

"*Oh love*" he said, as he put his arms around me. "*Has the dog died then?*"

He assumed I'd finished the story.

"*No. Not yet*" I gulped. "*But he is going to*".

I hadn't even got to the end of the book but I was anticipating the coming sorrow. I'm not sure I finished it or if I did I've blocked it from my memory.

There is an abundance of dog related events and exhibitions you can go to and in Basil's first year we tried out quite a few, obviously the fantastic Discover Dogs. We also ended up camping in a field in Windsor for two nights for something called Paws In The Park. Patrick spent a small fortune on a brand new tent, outdoor seating and camping and cooking gear. But it all came down to what we could stash in the car – which wasn't a great deal after we had managed to slot in three bottles of champagne.

I wasn't very happy at having to spend a couple of nights under canvas and the weather was looking grim. Basil was unsure of everything and skittered around nervously as we put the tent up. I knew he would be too nervous to sleep in the tent with us, and I was right. We hitched him to a pet spike dug into the ground and he curled up just under our awning, obviously keeping an eye out for any other dog who decided to come too close to his owners new, odd sleeping arrangements. Funnily enough I didn't sleep well either but then I've never been an 'outdoorsy' type of girl much to the disappointment of my husband.

We spent the day mooching round the varied dog related stalls, buying things we didn't need and signing up to some more dog charities. Naturally we kept an eye out for other Boxer owners and were happy to see many of the familiar shaped faces and bodies loping around. The sun came out and so did the jugs of Pimms and as we kicked off our shoes and sat back to watch the amazing doggy display teams I found this immersion in canine life wasn't so bad really.

Chapter 19: THE ENJOYING OF HOLIDAYS

One part of dog ownership I wasn't so sure about was the fact we were tied more to the home and less able to go on holiday. Foreign holidays seemed out of the question, after looking into pet passports and canine channel crossings it certainly seemed complicated. But one year when Basil was about two we decided to try out one of the 'dog-friendly' cottages you could hire in the countryside. We decided on a beautiful little house on the Suffolk coast in the middle of Summer and prepared to relax and enjoy ourselves.

After the four hour drive through congested East London and getting lost in the countryside, with Basil fretting on my lap the whole way – yes we were still stupidly driving the two-seater Porsche - we were all a bit crotchety. I continued to be fractious the next day when it dawned grey and rainy, I couldn't believe it, our first holiday in ages and it was going to be ruined, and all because we had a silly dog! It seemed terribly unfair as I imagined jumping on a last minute flight to somewhere sunny and gorgeous. I was used to beautiful hotels and beaches not hired houses and British weather.

Patrick vainly tried to raise our spirits and kept saying how happy Basil and he were at being away from London. And wasn't the area beautiful? He took us to the wet and windy beach and bought us all chips to cheer us up. A seagull knocked mine out of my hands and I could have cried. It was the last straw. But I knew I was being selfish and unfair. I had made the decision on creating this family and had to deal with the consequences. That night we found a beautiful little pub full of normal looking people all with their own dogs and none of them were crying. The three of us had a drunken laugh discussing the locals at the bar, our silly situation and how ridiculous I was!

The next day dawned beautiful and clear and it remained sunny and warm for the rest of our stay. We sunbathed, shopped, slept, explored, rambled, went for meals and were happy in the company of the three of us, exactly as a holiday should be. With not a room-service waiter or mini-bar in sight. We even signed up to stay for an extra couple of days.

Basil had a wonderful holiday, he discovered a love of eating cow pats – or 'flop snacks' as we named them. And for the first time we had a huge, huge garden he could run around in. He spent his time rolling around in the grass, pin-wheeling between the hedges and loving it. Once he went crashing straight through a high hedge and ended up in the field next door! He completely disappeared from sight. I heard him running on through the undergrowth. I stood up from my outdoor lunch worried. Would he come back? Should I run through the hedge after him? Then the sound of him clattering through the crops stopped. Silence. I waited. It started up again, got louder and suddenly Basil appeared again with some long grassy blades stuck to him. He'd obviously quickly realised he wasn't in the garden with him mum anymore, but decided that life on the other side wasn't for him and instead of taking his chance of freedom had panicked, turned round and come running back. Just in time for a sandwich.

But it wasn't just actual vacations that were altered, we had to make changes to how we celebrated seasonal holidays too. Basil's first Christmas was a real cause for celebration. We bought him lots of gifts and were excited at the thought of him opening them all up. (Patrick will tell you it's really hard to wrap a football). Basil was intrigued by the difference in the house, he really could tell something was up.

As usual we bought a large, natural tree and put it in a stand on the floor, every branch hung with glistening baubles, balls, tinsel and chains. Basil used to worry these, he would edge up to the tree and start nosing the balls closest to him. If they fell off he would chase them across the wooden floor, skittering along to try and get them into his mouth, covering his lips and snout with glitter and sometimes crushing the fragile globes into smithereens.

We started moving the lower hanging decorations higher up the tree. Basil started nosing up higher.

We moved more. He followed them up the tree. Eventually all of our decorations were hanging on the top half of the tree, which made for a rather lopsided effect. The next year we put the tree on a raised table, and still do.

As with every part of the dog world, there is a huge amount of related seasonal items you can purchase. And we bought all of them! The choc-drop advent calendar, the rawhide stocking, the canine Christmas card, the 'My First Christmas' food bowl, and that's not even going into Hallowe'en (doggy devil horns) or Easter (fluffy chick toys). As you can probably tell we are very keen observers of public holidays and private celebrations and Basil is at the heart of all of these occasions.

UNHAPPY CANINE DRACULA

Chapter 20: THE JOY OF COOKING

There is something attractive about dog food. I'm not sure what it is but it smells rather enticing sometimes (even though it is foul to have in your mouth) and I like mashing up little biscuits into it. I started to prepare Basil's food like I would Patrick's, trying to tempt him with little titbits and gently warming everything up, maybe with a drizzle of oil. He likes a small cheese starter sometimes to get his appetite going.

I would be despondent if he didn't eat everything, as if he didn't like my cooking, which is obviously ridiculous as I hadn't really prepared the tins of beefy stews myself (but is probably for the best as I am an appalling cook). I became, and still am, obsessed with him getting vitamins and vegetables so I mash them up into his food bowl, and I really have to mash them up well because Basil will always manage to find and delicately pick out even the tiniest bit of carrot, pea or broccoli, leaving little chains of vegetables in an otherwise licked clean bowl. He's quite clever and dextrous really. Patrick tells me it's because of his prehensile upper lip.

Despite not being able to rest if there is a bit of lamb in the slow cooker he's not overly obsessed by food. I know some dogs are completely driven by the need to track down and consume anything they can get their paws on. I remember a woman telling me about the time she had mistakenly left her kitchen door ajar, allowing her big Labrador to break in and scoff three whole loaves of bread. Three! Basil would have daintily turned his nose up at that, he only likes one or two slices spread with (real) butter.

Although one of his very early food habits really gave us a shock. As we couldn't go out as often in the evenings as we were used to during his puppy days, Patrick and I took to eating a lot of takeaways and convenience foods which we shared with Basil. He'd happily snap up discarded slices of pizza and tasty scraps and seemingly wander off to eat them, or so I thought. After the thawing of a bit of a cold snap we woke up in bed to find an excited, muddy Basil depositing a frozen black lump between us. Patrick extricated it from the sheets and held it up for inspection.

"*Is it coal?*" I asked, taking a sniff, "*where on earth has he got that from?*"
"*Hmmm, I don't think it's coal*" replied Patrick as he started crumbling the object between his fingers. Realisation hit and his face became horrified: "*Oh no, it's a bloody PORK PIE.*"

Disgusted, we both leapt out of the now grubby bed and raced into the garden. An old hole had obviously just been re-opened in the flower bed, it was lined with frozen pizza slices, bits of pitta bread and full of black cocktail sausages and the other half of the pork pie. Like an archaeological buffet, complete with maggots. We hadn't had party food like this for a while, not since we'd held a bit of a Halloween celebration a few months before. Basil had obviously stolen the snacks while we weren't looking and dug a special hole for them, supplementing it with any bits of takeaway offered to him and building up quite a hoard. We emptied the hole and covered it back up while Basil looked on, probably upset his secret squirrel stash had been discovered and destroyed. As long as it meant we weren't going to wake up to any more foodstuffs that needed carbon-dating he'd just have to live with it. Sorry boy.

We share a lot of our food with him, when buying ingredients for a roast dinner we always buy enough for three so Basil gets the same as us. One of his best delights is a bowl of cooked chicken with gravy (and of course the ubiquitous mashed up vegetables). Patrick will always give Basil the last bite of any sandwich that he has made *'because those are the rules'*, and the dog now certainly expects it! If the boys are home alone it's quite common for two plates of poached eggs and kippers with bread and butter to come out of the kitchen – one for each of them.

If we eat out we will always take any leftover meat home for Basil, wrapped up in a napkin and stashed in my handbag. The trick is to always remember that you have done this and give the 'doggy-bag' to your dog the moment you walk through the door. I've lost count of the amount of times I've looked in my handbag the morning after an evening out to find a slimy paper package filled with last night's uneaten lamb. Cold and stinking up everything else in there. It's like my drunken, forgotten chips all over again! Will I ever learn?

I'll never forget the time we took him to our newly found local dog-friendly pub and ordered three steaks off the menu. The barman didn't even blink an eye, asked how we would all like it cooked (Basil: medium rare) and his even arrived in a silver dog bowl ready chopped. Needless to say it became one of our favourite pubs and we often ordered a' la carte for Basil who developed a taste for their pitted olives and bread, but turned his nose up at their kind offers of dog biscuits. It's a far cry from drinking in Soho at 4am, but almost as much fun.

When I met Hugh Fearnley-Whittingstall at a cookery event of all the things I could have asked him, any culinary question on earth, I couldn't help but quiz him on what he fed his dog and asked if he had any tips for Basil and I. After looking at me for a second to check I wasn't mad (no just a bit drunk on organic nettle beer) he confessed to cooking up a few doggy treats himself and we happily discussed the merits of feeding fish to your pooch.

Basil's food cupboard is stuffed with not just dog tins and chews but steak and kidney puddings, jerky, sardines in oil and there is usually a rotisserie chicken, fresh liver and some stewing steak in the fridge. And when I bake cakes or biscuits he is always hanging around to lick out the mixing bowl.

I worry sometimes that he is ruined for basic dog food but thankfully if there is nothing human forthcoming from us he doesn't turn a can of chum down especially if its warmed up with some oil and cheese, which is a relief if you are too tired, hungover or drunk to oblige him with an egg sandwich.

Quite sweetly after he has eaten he regularly comes over to me for a little kiss and a cuddle, which I like to think is him coming to say thank you for his dinner. Patrick says he is just hanging around to see if there is any more, but I know better.

Chapter 21: THE STUDY OF ANATOMY

When Basil was a tiny puppy he was bitten or stung in the garden and came flying into the house yelping. He charged upstairs before we could grab him and hid under the bed shaking. We were totally at a loss what to do. Upset, we sat downstairs debating whether or not we should take him to the emergency vets (it was late at night) when a little face poked round the corner and with a worried lurch he leapt straight onto my chest and buried his head into my armpit. He lay there for a while shivering and whimpering.

This was a big turning in point in our relationship, I realised that we weren't just responsible for his physical needs (feeding, watering and cleaning up poo) but his emotional ones too. He came to me for comfort and reassurance, and I felt my heart expand with love at having such a responsibility for the little chap.

We did end up taking him to the vets (cue an amusing, fast and free late night taxi race across town). But by the time we arrived he was, of course, fine and didn't need the pain relieving jab he had, in fact he was doing his best cartwheels for the enchanted vet. All ended well, but I will never forget that night and how my view of owning a dog completely changed. I feel sorry for all of those dogs in the world who don't have the love, security and warmth of the 'forever home' they deserve. The owning of an innocent creature has certainly made me more emotional, sensitive and aware of wider problems. The only two charities I give to regularly are canine and childrens ones for this reason.

However much emotional security and love we give Basil, he gives it right back. I swear he can tell if you are anxious or upset or even in discomfort. One particularly grim day I was sitting on the sofa in pain, enduring what eventually turned out to be a miscarriage. I was confused and hurting and waiting to speak to a duty doctor and Basil just sat with me for hours. Very still, his head rested in my lap, he wouldn't leave my side and didn't pester me once for playtime, a ball or a treat as he usually would. As Patrick couldn't be with me that day the comfort I got from Basil made me realise that he really was a member of my family – and one I could rely on.

But he can be a bit obsessed with us. When walking with Patrick and I, if we split up for whatever reason (usually when I am lagging behind on a run), Basil will attempt to keep equidistant between us. He has to know where everyone is at all times. He anxiously herds us around the house too, if one of us is on the top floor and the other on the ground floor, Basil is right in the middle unable to rest until we are all in the same room. I think he is only really happy when the three of us are in bed and he can lay on top of both of us, keeping us in check.

Basil has been in hospital for overnight stays twice and I was a wreck both times. The second time I had to leave work early (leaving an email to the team asking them to *pray for my boy*) just to be nearer the hospital. I hate the little shaved patch he gets on his front leg where a drip has been inserted, for some reason it makes him look even more pitiable. It's like they do it on purpose to make the owners feel worse when their dogs are bought out after their ops and all shaky on their paws. They are led out from behind closed doors and make a sad attempt to jump up at you with usual gusto - but just can't make it. It's terrible. Basil always looks at us stoically as if to say: *'Don't worry, I was ok, I got through it – just about'*. I remember after his castration he was so wobbly he was careering off walls all evening before collapsing in an undignified heap.

He recently had to be stitched up after a nasty cut on his leg, we went to pick him up at the end of the day and as usual he came wobbling out trying to jump up to kiss us but just not managing it. The kindly nurse bent down to put the large plastic cone on his head (to stop him worrying his stitches) and he promptly passed out. Honestly I'd never seen anything so pathetic.

Dogs wearing cones get a lot of attention. Apart from the fact your dog looks like he is wearing a plastic lampshade it is a signal to everyone else that they have been injured and there will be a few extra strokes and smiles as you walk along (and the obligatory question about *'picking up SkySports on that thing'* from a friend). But you also look ridiculous! Passers-by who have no idea why your dog should be wearing such a thing just laugh at you. I'll admit it is pretty funny, especially when they walk into a lamp-post. I am guilty of laughing at my own dog as he tried to walk down the road wearing one and got his head stuck in a gate.

Thankfully he's never had a serious accident or really been that ill, apart from the time he got gastroenteritis from drinking a puddle in Primrose Hill, and he has just had an infected anal gland squeezed (but I am just unable to talk about that experience).

However, I remember one funny day we were taking a stroll around Camden and on taking the tow path along the canal the still young Basil took it upon himself to run into the water. He just started sprinting and carried on off the edge. He didn't even jump. He just kind of disappeared. Patrick had him on an extending lead so he wasn't hampered in his lemming attempt. He was completely submerged!

But I could see the line of the lead disappearing into the water, so rushing up I grabbed at it and with one hand raised a spinning, sopping puppy into the air. I'm not sure who was most surprised? All three of us surveyed each other: Patrick standing shocked, still holding the handle of the lead, me balancing on the canal edge holding our dog aloft (the thin cord burning into my hand with the weight of him) or the slowly turning Basil who ruefully looked down at the disappearing ground that wasn't meant to turn into this watery stuff. We quickly bundled the shivering dog home and wrapped him in a warm towel. Silly boy.

Basil has joint medication administered as a gravy flavour juice in his food. Flea treatments are given when we remember or are feeling a bit itchy, (but usually when we spring clean the house, have someone over to the house or move house). And all tablets are given in a little lump of cheap cheese – you know what they say about a spoonful of sugar helping the medicine go down? Well, it's the same for dogs!

We still take him for regular check-ups and booster jabs, we all view it as a little family outing and best clothes are always worn. We chat with the vets in a slightly posher accent and try to subconsciously reassure them that we are responsible pet owners by asking plenty of needless questions about feeding and heart murmurs as we all nod knowledgably and smile lots.

You'll get to know your dog's body very well, usually because it's always lying on top of you, but this is a good thing because you can tell when something is up with them. In our house we have various descriptions for bits of Basil or the things he does, which would mean that anyone listening in to one of our conversations might be slightly confused as only Patrick and I know what they mean. Basil shorthand if you will.

Here are some examples and best not used when you're at the vets:

- WIGGUNS – his soft ears

- MUSHROOM – when he curls himself up really small to make a circle shape (as in not taking up 'much room')
- BEST IN SHOW – his noble stance
- HAMS – his lovely well turned thighs
- PYJAMA CASE – a little ruff of fur that travels up his chest and looks like a zip
- VELVET PURSE – his saggy, soft chops (also known as SATCHMO)
- LOPSIDED LIPPIES – where his bottom lips hangs further down on one side
- ROLLED UP SOCK – one of his white paws extends further up the leg than the others
- THE TAP END – getting his paws and claws facing you during a cuddle, like getting the taps in the back of your head during a shared bath
- THUMB TAIL – the nub of Basil's docked tail looks like a thumb
- SHOVEL FACE – when he stands over you his chops hang down in a square giving the odd impression of a face shape reminiscent of a shovel

Chapter 22: THE PURSUIT OF FAME

Working in Public Relations I deal closely with media and am friends with plenty of journalists – especially trade press writers who report on our industry. I have been interviewed and quoted myself but after getting a mention for Basil in one of our trade papers I thought it was time for my little boy to get in on the act too, rather like a canine version of Mrs Worthington or Pushy Mother. My business partner mentioned him in an interview and I bombarded the press with information about his birthday party only half jokily.

But the best was yet to come – a good friend worked on the UK's best-selling film magazine, Empire, and in return for a readers letter was happy to print a picture of Basil wearing a Superman t-shirt in the Editor's Letters page. I couldn't have been happier and think I have about three copies of Basil's issue at home. And a great picture of him is also filed in the picture library of a major publishing house just in case a picture of 'a dog' is needed. Maybe it's true that every dog has its day and we'll see him posing properly in a magazine or catalogue one day?

One sunny afternoon wc were approached in the street by a rather dapper fellow outside Camden market. He mentioned that he had seen us around and had a shop selling pet clothes, would we be interested in Basil being a model as he was *'gorgeous'* and *'so full of character'*. Interested? Now I know this was hardly the same as the discovery of Kate Moss, but I honestly couldn't have been prouder!

I'm not sure why I should be surprised, he has a noble lineage. Despite my earlier dismissal of hearing that Basil had Crufts winners in his line, sure enough when his pedigree certificate arrived from the Kennel Club we were impressed to see that he has no fewer than 15 winners in his past five generations. I am not a huge believer in this selective and proud breeding process that results in dogs being considered 'suitable' or not but we still proudly display that certificate in a frame on the wall (*Fletch's Flyer* indeed!). He'll never go to Crufts or competitively take part in real dog shows but we were proud enough when he won 'Most Handsome Dog' at a little local event held at a park up the road. We cheered him on with beers and hung the rosette on the wall.

Sadly there aren't many famous Boxer Dogs, which is a shame because they do look so noble. But we did once see Simon Callow walking through Camden with a fine pair of reds – we nodded to him in a *'we own boxers'* kind of way – and after a brief chat about the more engaging qualities of the breed we felt that Basil had a little brush with stardom through association.

Local singer Amy Winehouse lived right behind us and often on our walks around the little streets we would end up going past her house. The cobbles were always packed with fans hoping for a glimpse of her and paparazzi hoping for a lucrative photograph. While I would walk past with my head in the air, tut-tutting at them for taking up all the space and making it unpleasant for locals (the area was always ankle deep in the photographers' fag-butts) Basil would growl and sniff and make it very clear that they were not welcome. A very perceptive dog our boy.

He's also such a handsome lad we arranged for him to have his own photo shoot! A special 'Animal Photographer' was booked who we had met and vetted at a Dog Exhibition we'd attended. She specialised in dogs and cajoled Basil into all sorts of positions with his ball in Regent's Park and in the front seat of our Boxster, the results of which can still be seen on our walls today. But she also had a special purpose for coming to see us... sadly Basil would be unable to attend our wedding in person, but we wanted him there in spirit – a huge photo of him at the event would ensure this happened. So she duly snapped him wearing a bow tie and looking very smart so he could be there as a 'virtual guest'.

WHAT A HANDSOME BOY

Chapter 23: THE SAYING OF THE VOWS

We had to get Basil ready for his three weeks away in the Dog Hotel. I was incredibly excited about our wedding and honeymoon but I knew we would miss him and that he would miss us. For days beforehand it was like the elephant in the room, *The Dropping off of Basil* wasn't discussed right up until the morning we actually had to do it.

We knew where we were going, we had been there twice before to let Basil get used to the place and check out the facilities and owners. It was a rather nice secluded cottage in Kentish woods inhabited by a well-to-do retired couple and their three black Labradors. These weren't kennels by any stretch of the imagination, rather The Paw Seasons for dogs.

I had done a lot of research online beforehand. There were even some Dog Hotels that had web-cams so you could view your little furry friend online no matter how far away from home you were. Believe me if we could have found one of those places closer to us that's where he would have gone! But then I imagine we'd have spent our honeymoon obsessively searching for Wi-Fi in the Indian Ocean in order to see some grainy images of Basil having a snooze.

But our chosen carers had promised us that he would text us while we were away just to keep us up to date with his activities – yes text us. (And when those bleeping messages came in I really did believe they were from Basil himself and it made me feel a whole lot better to hear that *'I've been for a long walk today mummy and am now just having my tea'* whilst we were sunbathing in the Maldives).

We turned off into the long narrow driveway leading to Basil's holiday home. Taking us deeper and deeper into the countryside. The air was full of unfamiliar smells that day and the fields full of pheasants. The affect it had on Basil was incredible and he suddenly abandoned his sophisticated Soho persona. He, usually happy to relax in my lap or the footwell as we drove along, started struggling to get out of the car, he fought and fought and it was all I could do to hold him in. We had the soft top down on account of the sunshine but had to pull over in order to put it back up. His little scrabbling claws were tearing at my arms so desperate was he to answer the call of the wild.

He's not normally sway to his animalistic ways but we honestly nearly lost him to the countryside that day. If he could have made it out of the car I swear we would have never seen him again and probably heard reports years later of a feral hound inhabiting the woods and living with pheasants. Despite having had him for nearly two years it was a completely unknown dog I held nervously in my arms for the rest of the way.

Soon he was deposited in his temporary home and after many backward glances Patrick and I were alone and on our way again. This time towards a new chapter in our lives, our marriage. In just two days' time we would be at our own wedding and I couldn't believe it. It was with some dismay I looked down to discover that my arms had started to bruise from Basil's flurry of bird-related activity and in my sleeveless dress those would definitely show up on the big day. Grrrr... Bad boy!

I was incredibly nervous on my wedding day. I could barely eat a thing, which made a change - I had been celebrating my impending nuptials so often I must have been the only bride to put weight on before her big day! I was also slightly hungover from a rather raucous dinner with my two girlfriends the night before. We were all slightly worse for wear despite our best efforts to keep things low key. But a blissful massage and manicure in Harrods followed by a session with a hairdresser and make-up artist (and a few glasses of champagne of course) soon sorted me out.

Our beautiful wedding venue was in Knightsbridge, the grand walls were hung with portraits of noble folk long since dead, and beside them was a large canvas of Basil looking smart in his bow-tie. As I stood upstairs I could hear my friends and family congregate below me and waiting for proceedings to start. I was left alone with only his picture for company and seeing Basil look down at me, his cute, eager face all alive with happiness I was momentarily calmed and thankful for the presence of his familiar love.

I didn't have any doubts about what I was doing but I was considering how far we had come and how much I had changed. It seemed that the former girl-about-town had been tamed. For a hen night present I had been presented with my very own Empire magazine front cover by a wonderful friend who worked there – the headline read *'Her Party Days Are Over'*. Was that true? Had I really done everything exciting that I was going to do? Was that what marriage meant? Were my party days going to be over?

I was lucky enough to have lived what I considered to be an exciting life. I had:

- Set up my own business before the age of 30
- Lived on £5 a week as a student
- Stayed up for 48hours partying in Singapore
- Snorkelled over a shipwreck in Bermuda
- Been a centrefold model in a magazine
- Met more than one James Bond
- Discovered myself at festivals and lost myself at raves
- Shopped in New York, Miami and Dubai

- Fallen in love with Paris and fallen in love in Rome
- Received the attentions of a world famous film-star
- Seen a live sex show in Amsterdam and a total eclipse of the sun in Munich
- Stayed in some of the world's most beautiful hotels, sometimes alone, sometimes not
- Slept under the stars with a man I had only just met
- Walked up more red carpets than I could remember
- Partied with soap stars, film stars and on one memorable night a controversial artist who got me into a party just because our boobs were the same size!

But I knew I was bored of the travelling and staying out late, I missed Patrick and Basil far too much. I was sometimes happier watching EastEnders with a bottle of wine than attending the screening of a new film (even with free champagne thrown in). I knew I could happily take the plunge. And besides I could still pick and choose what events I attended. We could still go out, but for now I was prepared to throw myself into this new chapter in my life. I wasn't going to be the oldest swinger in town! I took a deep breath and walked down the stairs towards my groom.

Our wedding was a joyous affair, full of fun, laughter and love, exactly as it should have been and Basil was mentioned many times, including in the speeches. Everyone loved his portrait and we had plenty of photos taken with it, one of our favourites being the two of us holding the portrait close to us, it really looks as if our dog was a guest in the room. Most of the pictures also show up a few rather large bruises on my arm (thanks boy!) and when I look at the wedding album now I laugh and remember Basil trying to run away with the pheasants.

LOOK AT THE BRUISE ON MY ARM!

Chapter 24: THE AGONY OF ABSENCE

The Maldives are boring. Yes, I know how lucky I am to have experienced such a place and it sounds incredibly selfish, especially after complaining so much and fighting so hard for my freedom and an easy, glamorous life. But I am sorry, it is. It is absolutely beautiful and peaceful and romantic and all of those things you imagine, but we couldn't help thinking that if we were to have this chance to travel knowing that Basil was being taken care of we would have preferred to have spent the cash on cocktails and shopping in New York. Believe me for what we had spent on two weeks in our island paradise we could have lived it up fine style in the Big Apple for a week and had a far better time (and maybe bought home some decent new clothes instead of a pair of flip-flops and a shark-tooth pendant).

Because really the same tiny island beach is the same tiny island beach day after day, the only difference being what book you are reading or what you are going to have for dinner in the limited amount of restaurants your resort has to offer. The only interaction with other human beings is asking the cocktail waiter for another drink and the obsessive checking out of other women's ring fingers upon arrival at the airport (I kid you not. It took me ages to realise why so many women were trying to get a look at my left hand!). Oh and throw in the odd boat trip and massage.

It sounds idyllic to some but after a couple of years of kicking back and becoming more homely I felt we should have grabbed the bull by the honeymoon horns and done something outrageous. Despite having travelled to some lovely places separately we had never really spent much time abroad together and now we had Basil to look after we doubted we would ever really get the chance again. And funnily enough I didn't get on a plane for years after that holiday.

Despite receiving texts from Basil we both missed him terribly. It was while we were on our honeymoon that I started thinking about his exploits and writing them down (the result of which is what you are reading here). I dreamt about him loads and remembered in minute detail all of his early experiences. After spending two years of our life with him a three week absence was a hard term, despite the fact we were enjoying our first weeks of married life very much and almost guiltily revelling in having a large, empty (clean) bed to ourselves.

We had been apart from Basil for a couple of nights before that however. A year or so before we had decided to go to Spain for a couple of nights to visit my grandmother who was staying there. Thankfully a couple of good friends and dog lovers agreed to have him for us. We were worried (for all three of them) but were incredibly grateful and knew that no harm could come to any of them in such a short space of time. We left a lot of food for him (the steak & kidney puddings were sniffed at by the resident vegetarian who refused to believe they were actually intended for human consumption) and a list of instructions which included him not being walked off the lead or sleeping on their bed.

That first night Patrick, my Nan and I had a high old time, laughing at the hotel's ridiculous cabaret, drinking sangria and dancing. We did spare a though for Basil and our friends and texted to ask if everything was alright? Immediately two photos were sent back, the first showed Basil running as free as you like through Richmond Park, not a lead in sight. The second was of the three of them tucked up in bed together. Maybe they hadn't had time to read the instructions I'd left?

And I had been away from Basil by myself a few times too. A work trip had seen me having to spend a few days in Dubai acting as a publicist for a rather impulsive movie star during a busy film festival. After a pressurized few days with very little sleep I was glad to be on the plane home, and quite literally fell through the door in tears so relieved was I to be back with the family. And Basil nearly danced himself dizzy with relief to see me in return.

And a few weeks before the wedding I had a pre-nuptials break in Florida with my best friends. A sun-drenched, extended hen-do if you will. Another friend had lent us his house and the four of us had some happy days laughing in the pool and visiting the local bars, beach and crab shack. We also managed a magical night in Miami drinking dreamy cocktails in huge beds by the side of a sparkling pool into the small hours...

But despite being in America's 'Sunshine State' I still missed Basil. Patrick texted me a small photo of him to accompany me on my trip, I saved it as my phone wallpaper so I could look at it constantly. I didn't even mind that he was pictured wrapped up in my best Laura Ashley toile bed linen, which ordinarily I'd have been furious about. My friend bought him a fluffy alligator as a present on the way home.

Chapter 25: THE BUN IN THE OVEN

The honeymoon was finally over. We landed late the night before but were up early to go and pick up our boy. Jet lag be damned! We were so excited to see him again. Would he recognise us? Would he remember us? Would he have an inkling that his mum and dad were now married and he was part of an official family unit? We certainly felt like a proper little family now we just need to collect Basil to make ourselves whole again. But there was definitely something amiss that morning...

We had left the house early enough so we could stop off at some motorway services for breakfast. But something surreal had obviously happened to us while we were scoffing bacon and eggs, because when we got on the road again we headed off the wrong way around the M25. Then we just couldn't either get off the motorway at the right exit or seem to go in the right direction and suddenly there seemed to be traffic everywhere. We felt like screaming! What was going on? Why were we being kept from our happy canine reunion?

After what seemed like hours, and certainly a long time since we had gotten out of bed, we eventually pulled up at the agreed meeting place very late indeed. Basil's temporary carer was waiting for us in a small country car-park. Everyone seemed to leap out of their car seat at the same time to greet each other – including Basil! But he was a very different looking dog from the one we had dropped off three weeks ago. This skinny, skittish dog wasn't our robust, bonny boy. He was emaciated!

Sadly, it seemed that Basil had gone on hunger strike in protest at being left in this gorgeous country spot with other doggy friends, having long walks in smelly woods every day, with treats and cuddles on hand. Yes, our lad obviously preferred our basement flat in Camden with its little square garden and sometimes only having a walk to the local pub. In a way I was secretly pleased that he had nearly pined away for us.

But it was sad to see him like that, as it turned out he had gone off his food and he didn't take kindly to having to share a bowl with other hounds. He's particular in that respect, every other dog I have ever met is happy to eat or drink from any dog bowl, certainly every canine visitor that comes to my home greedily helps themselves to whatever is on offer. But Basil always turns his nose up at anything communal. It's hard when we go to places that kindly leave out water bowls for dogs, we either have to ask for our own personal one or I will sneak it into the toilets and wash it up and fill with fresh water before offering it to him because he is so fussy. I am sure if he could wash his paws after tumbling around with other dogs he would, as it is he is constantly cleaning his bits and pieces. As I say he is quite particular.

The hotel owner actually asked us for more money to pay for extra food as it seems we hadn't supplied enough. Being English and awkward I immediately wrote her out a cheque for the new amount, when I should have been pointing out that it was quite patently obvious that any dog staying in the hotel apart from Basil had been eating his food, and he certainly hadn't had anything extra. Internally I seethed at the thought of her dogs getting fatter on all the little tins of sardines and tripe we had left behind for Basil to eat, while he sadly moped in the corner unable to stomach a mouthful.

Soon enough we were on our way back home, a wedded threesome looking forward to starting our new married life together. Basil slept all the way home on my lap in the car, he then slept for about 24 hours in his own bed, he then woke up and had a huge meal from his own clean bowl. Patrick and I watched over him like worried parents as he still seemed unhappy, but we nursed him back to his full fighting weight within days. It took a lot longer than that though for him to forgive us and it was over a week before he came to us unprompted for a cuddle. We vowed never again to leave him for so long. And besides, travel was unlikely for some time because soon enough I was pregnant.

I can remember the exact night we conceived. We'd been on a fantastic night out to the old Camden Palace to see another friend DJ. I'd worn some fabulous shoes, electric blue with silver high heels. Sadly they were rather painful to dance in and I didn't want to walk home in them, after complaining and having a bit of a row with Patrick over wearing shoes I couldn't walk in (what girl doesn't have a pair of shoes that will only just about take her from a cab to a bar-stool?) he ripped them off my feet and made me walk home without them. I wasn't happy but as I waddled along freezing I saw the funny side and we soon made up. Yes, that was definitely the night!

The morning after I saw the blue and silver shoes on the floor, Basil had chewed them up. Well at least they wouldn't be causing any more rows between Patrick and I. As I stared at them I wondered... and only three nights later I was sure. We were out for dinner at the Oxo Tower (one of our favourite restaurants in town with beautiful views along the river, it's a place we often went to for celebrations and somewhere I regularly used for entertaining local magazine editors) and as we went up in the lift I felt a wave of nausea and light-headedness. Now, I am rather claustrophobic and hate being in lifts, but I knew it wasn't that. I think I just knew!

I had a mixed experience of pregnancy. Sadly, it had taken us a couple of tries to go full term but I like to view these now as 'trial runs' for what turned out to be our perfect baby in the end. I was happy to be pregnant. I liked the feel of a hardening bump under the fleshy tummy I had cultivated from years of drinking and eating out. And I was relieved that my propensity for throwing up while hungover hadn't extended to pregnancy and I managed to avoid any real morning sickness.

But I also found the process to be confusing and full of unnecessary intervention. Almost from day one there seemed to be the potential of a problem. Every visit to the doctor, midwife or hospital revealed I was in danger of developing 'something', I had tests for 'everything' and all of them revealed 'nothing'. It felt like we could never really relax and enjoy the experience because we were concerned about the next possible problem on the horizon.

Even the magical scan that revealed the sex (we were having a boy and I was overjoyed, because as I say there is room for only one princess in my home) revealed the possibility of an impending difficulty, which was a shame as it ruined our temporary happiness. Of course I know they have to take very good care with pregnant women but in reality my baby and I were healthy all the way through the pregnancy and if I hadn't seen one medical professional from conception to birth I might have enjoyed the whole thing a bit more.

And we were a bit stranded at home. Again! In our two-seater car Basil had to sit in the footwell, he had to stop sitting on my lap as it started to disappear. Eventually Basil disappeared from view too as my tummy took over, and it became unfair for all three (four) of us to travel around like that sadly. Which meant if we couldn't take public transport or walk we couldn't really go anywhere together.

One symptom of pregnancy though actually affected my relationship with Basil. I was always grateful he was around when I was feeling weepy or unsure and used to enjoy his cuddles as usual, until one day I noticed he smelt a bit funny. Actually he smelt terrible!

"Patrick, we need to do something about Bas, he stinks. Can we give him a bath?"

"He smells ok to me?" he replied taking a good sniff.

"Honestly, can you not smell that?" I was incredulous, it was so pungent.

"Honestly, no I can't but we'll give him a bath if you like"

Poor Basil was hauled up for an unexpected bath, completely indignant because he hadn't even been rolling in mud for a change. Patrick had to do the honours because I couldn't go near him.

"Ah that's better" I said, as a while later the two of them came downstairs slightly damp. *"Oh no, it's not, take him outside to dry, its clinging to him"*

"Alice, he's fine, he smells of nothing but shampoo now"

But to me the air was full of this acrid, hot smell of intense doggyness, I couldn't tolerate it. *"Please please just put him outside for a bit"* I pleaded.

Now normally we think our dog smells gorgeous and sometimes the most comforting thing in the world is to get a sniff of him. He has the aroma of warm freshly baked ginger biscuits usually, unless he has been running hard and rolling in a muddy puddle after which he can get a bit 'rabbit hutchy'. But he always smells warm and alive to us, even his ears smell like honey. We do worry sometimes that he can make our home a bit 'doggy like' to visitors and we have all manner of carpet sprays and air fresheners that claim to take it away. Because we live with him we don't notice the smell and always worry that when someone comes round they will leave with *'yes, nice people but they could do with washing that dog a bit more often'* on their lips.

Oh dear, it seemed that my pregnancy meant I was experiencing some kind of heightened smell but only in relation to the dog. He reeked! I could hardly bear to be in the same room as him, how long would this last? Would I ever be able touch my dog again?

We went to the pet shop and bought every kind of anti-smell potion we could find, all flavoured with evening-primrose oil and anti-bacterial ingredients and the like. That poor dog was washed, brushed, sprayed and rubbed to within an inch of his life.

Nothing worked. He had to move out of the bedroom as I couldn't get a wink of sleep – my nose wrinkling in the dark as he snoozed near me. He was pushed off the sofa and couldn't go near any clothes or cushions in case he contaminated things with his horrific smell.

After a couple of weeks we were all at our wit's end. But I started to notice a subtle change, something else was taking over, I was now desperate to smell vinegar and found that helped with the smell of Basil. In fact I could cope with it. Mmmm lovely vinegar, if I could just keep it near me I couldn't smell the dog. I quickly progressed from smelling it to putting it on my food, all of my food, on everything I could. I loved it, couldn't get enough of it, I ate pickled onions by the handful. My thoughts were consumed with vinegar, not fancy stuff, not balsamic or raspberry but proper old brown malt. Soon I was drinking it straight. I could think of nothing nicer than sitting on the sofa with a big bowl of brown vinegar with some bits of bread to dip in it followed by slurping up the rest. I must have stunk worse than the dog? Basil would curl up on my feet and look at his weird mummy. Happily, I couldn't smell him at all anymore.

HE'S NEVER BEEN A FAN OF THE BATH

If there was one real medical problem with my pregnancy, and it's not really a problem, it was that my baby was a big one. In fact he was huge; he turned out to be nearly 11lbs huge. It made for a rather uncomfortable last couple of months. Now I am no fragile girl but it was tough. I honestly looked like I had swallowed a space hopper. I feared my body would never be the same again (and I was right).

Sleeping the three of us on the bed, in reality four, was becoming harder and harder as I tried to find a comfortable space for my huge self. If I *could* get to sleep I would wake up in the early hours, gasping for breath. An intense, claustrophobic feeling would steal over me as my huge host-body felt overwhelmed by this growing parasite. I couldn't lie down, I couldn't sit up, I couldn't get away from it. I'd have to get out of the dark bedroom and stagger downstairs to run my wrists, thundering with hot and worried blood, under the cold tap and splash my face. Usually I would end up in the lounge knowing that there was no chance of sleep again that night. Trying to calm down and get my breath back I would have to get on all fours to pull the weight down off my lungs.

A little noise would let me know that Basil was also on his way down stairs to see what was up. Again I was thankful for his company, he would come over and sniff my face as I crouched on the floor, then get onto the sofa to watch me. As soon as I was calm again and able to breathe I would go and join him. The two of us would then sit up cuddling until first light watching late night TV or listening to the radio. He'd even rest his head on my huge bump. Thank you boy.

I was still taking Basil to work with me at this point and we'd walk as far as I could from my home to the office. An absolutely massive pregnant woman with her big handbag and her large dog all trotting along. I was acutely aware that while I was in charge of two precious lives I was completely incapable of protecting any of us, I was so vulnerable and unwieldy. But still, I was supremely happy and as always reassured by the presence of my dog who thankfully never pulled me off my feet, I'd have gone down like a ton of bricks.

My due date came and went but baby and I kept on growing. And growing. My doctors were concerned (of course) and suggested that I needed to be induced sooner rather than later because the larger he got the harder it would be on the big day. No kidding!

Soon enough the day came and soon enough our son Stanley was born. And once again our lives were to change. If I had any doubts about being part of a family before, there was really no going back this time. Would this baby fit into our lives as well as the dog had? I knew you could just about stash a dog under a bar stool, but a Moses basket? Probably not so much. And you really can't leave kiddies in kennels for three weeks can you? Not even really nice ones with webcams.

Chapter 26: THE MAKING OF A MOTHER

As a new mum to a baby I was surprised how similar it was to my early fears and feelings of owning Basil. (Obviously the procedure of delivering my human baby was a lot more painful than picking up Basil in the car, but now I understood why his poor mother had looked so miserable in that field that day – she'd produced a litter of six, and probably a lot more besides. I vowed to stop at one!) But I certainly remembered those early feelings of frustration and claustrophobia at being bound to the house by a little needy charge, alongside the intense feelings of love and amazement at this lovely little body we had created.

I resented Basil hugely while I was in hospital because I was desperate for my husband to spend more time with us there, because we'd had quite a difficult birth we had to stay in for a very long week. (I wore my Boxer print pyjamas the whole time of course). But Patrick was so worried about Basil continuing with his normal routine that he kept going home after just a couple of hours visiting.

"*But he's only a bloody dog*" I would whine unfairly (something I know I would never have said before). Would the baby change how I felt about our dog? Patrick was rightly concerned.

Of course Patrick was right, he should continue to treat Basil as he always had been treated: our number one boy. It certainly wouldn't be fair to completely change his status in the house, although I know I am guilty of changing my focus and being more exasperated by the extra work a dog gives you when you are already stressed out and exhausted from having a new baby. He just seemed like such hard work and a distraction at this time.

Stanley had finally landed in the house, but Basil wasn't even interested. I think he was concerned that I had been away for so long and worried that daddy had been away a lot, but he didn't really acknowledge the baby when he eventually arrived in his new home.

I was focussed almost solely on Stanley but for the first few weeks Patrick couldn't see the attraction at all. He did everything completely right - he changed nappies, helped with night feeds, took him for walks but we both knew he wasn't yet in love with our new addition. *"It's like having to look after the neighbour's cat"* he would say and I would cry and not just because I was still hormonal.

Patrick and Basil really bonded again at this time and went on a lot of long walks together. Probably finding solace in each other's company from the mad woman who had landed in their previously quiet home with a screaming infant in tow. I believe Patrick felt he had lost me for a while and in a suddenly spinning world Basil was the only stationary point he could focus on. Always loving, dependable and ready for a walk with a ball, that dog really helped him through a tough and lonely patch.

This was a dark and frustrating period for us all. I was disproportionally upset by dog hairs on baby clothes and bedding, I felt it unhealthy for all four of us to sleep in one bedroom and I even resented Basil watching me breast-feed for some reason. And when he barked at the doorbell as usual and woke the baby up from a nap - disturbing any precious time I had to myself - I could have absolutely killed him.

Walking Basil with Stanley strapped to me in a baby harness felt dangerous and I was constantly scared while pushing the pushchair with Basil attached to the handle (something that you are told quite rightly never to do) that he would hare off down the street pulling the baby under a car. But I didn't know how else to walk him while pushing a heavy buggy.

I often thought about just leaving the front door open 'by mistake' and seeing what would happen... maybe Basil would just walk out and disappear? But of course I knew even if I did he would never leave us, he'd never leave home no matter how bad things got.

Yes, to say it was a bit of an odd time is an understatement. I really wasn't sure what I was doing and everything felt just too hard. Patrick came home one day to find me on Camden Council's website, looking up 'Adoption'. He was surprised.

"What are you looking at adoption for?" he asked.
"We've only just had a baby"
"I don't want to adopt another one" I replied grimly. *"I want to give this one away but I can't find anywhere on this site that will tell me how to do it"'*
He shut the computer down and made me a cup of tea.

I didn't realise I was mourning my previous life, the life I had only just got back together after the arrival of Basil had disrupted it. And I probably was a bit depressed. I couldn't begin to think where my next creative outlet would come from: a part of my life and career that had been so important to me. I certainly couldn't imagine when I would next feel free or even happy. The only thing I could control was my baby and I held him close to me and didn't let anyone else in for a while.

Sadly it meant that my previously adored hound was largely ignored by me during this time, he wandered around the house sniffing his empty food bowl or with a sigh slept alone upstairs. I didn't recognise that the sensible rhythm of the house that so suited the baby had been established because of our dog. My natural instinct to protect and nurture had flourished with his ownership and despite considering myself a new mum, the reality was I had already been a mother. We already had experience in caring for a young life and I should have trusted better that in a way we already knew what we were doing. And of course, I was already completely comfortable with cleaning up poo and sick.

I could rely on the fact that as I sat up in the pitch-black bedroom dealing with baby feeds throughout the night (so tired I would be dreaming with my eyes open) Basil would be awake too, watching me in the dark. Always there, always reassuring. He stayed awake with me even when Patrick continued sleeping. How could I continue resenting him?

Of course it wasn't long before Patrick and Stanley suddenly clicked, joyously and beautifully. Two pairs of exactly the same eyes looked at each other and recognised each other. I was happy. I didn't need to begrudge Basil anymore because Patrick had made room for our new baby in the house and his life. We threw ourselves into parenthood and once again life in our house changed, for the better.

Soon the four of us were on those long walks together and I have many happy memories of us trundling round Regent's Park with a new pushchair that cost the same as my first car and stopping for cups of coffee and cuddles. I wasn't so happy the day Patrick kicked a football for Basil and it landed directly in said pushchair, bouncing squarely off of Stanley's little squished face making him scream, but you get the idea.

After a while I began to realise that much like dog ownership having a child came with its own set of idiosyncrasies and so here are my top ten signs that show you're definitely a mother (of a human baby):

1. You can move silently from the top to the bottom of your home, avoiding every creaking floorboard or step - even in the dark. You can communicate without uttering a sound and know the quietest cycles on your washing machine and dishwasher. For some reason no-one else seems to be able to do

this and they continue to walk and talk normally (or think it's ok have a play wrestle with the dog right outside baby's bedroom!)

2. You have a drawer stuffed full of bras of differing shapes and sizes, but probably only about one or two fit you right now. I've probably changed bra size about five times in the last five years! I laugh so much when I read interviews with pregnant celebrities who say *'me and my partner really love my boobs right now'* because they have no idea that in a year from now when the baby is out and the breastfeeding is done they'll be left with a 25% volume loss and a completely unrecognisable chest (and about 50 unwearable bras).

3. Your life is full of unfinished cups of tea and conversations. You make a great cuppa or you start talking to someone but are immediately distracted by your offspring about to do something dangerous, so the tea goes undrunk and words go unsaid.

4. You spend a lot of time bending up and down picking things up from the floor. And after nine

months of pregnancy and probably a difficult labour you know for sure that your back will never be the same again. Same goes for your pelvic floor, breasts and memory. (Also my feet are now a size larger – what's that about?)

5. You can talk to other mums at Baby Group and happily ignore that smell of baby sick that seems to be following you around because you assume it can't be you until you get home and realise you have a massive splatter all down your top. You can also do a full town-centre shop still wearing the gaudy sticker on your chest that you got from Baby Gym proudly displaying your name in a colourful clown face to every shop assistant and bus driver. Your baby has cleverly taken theirs off to avoid such embarrassment.

6. Previously precious or coveted items such as mobile phones, keys, cameras, iPods and remote controls are willingly handed over to your child if it means they are entertained for five minutes. Even though you know they'll get all gummed up.

7. You haven't slept for a straight 8 hours since you gave birth, and if you were due in Summer, carrying a large baby or worried about labour then the chances are it's been a lot longer.

8. You dread being ill more than normal. Pre-baby you used to be able to take the day off work to lie on the sofa in a duvet watching This Morning with a cup of hot chocolate and wait for the sickness to pass (cuddling your sympathetic pooch if you have one). Now, no matter how much you are sweating, shivering or swooning that baby still needs to fed, watered, changed and entertained - and even if you can't stand up without wanting to fall over you still have to pick that baby up and put it somewhere safe before you run to the loo for an emergency. Perversely you have never been sicker since you had a child and now seem to pick up every bug going. And not only do mothers not get sick leave we also don't have lunch breaks, fag breaks, spontaneous cake breaks or Dress Down Friday.

9. You will happily suck the snot out of your baby's nose if it means someone gets some sleep. You will

also (again happily) let your teething child bite your fingers really hard if it affords them some relief from the pain and you some from the noisy tears.

10. You feel guilty about something every single day, and usually tense and worried too. When you lay down to sleep you can't - not because you're not utterly exhausted - but because your shoulders are locked up around your ears and your teeth are permanently gritted. If you do get some sleep you feel guilty.

Motherhood sure is a wonderful thing...

Chapter 27: THE MARCHING OF TIME

We left London and moved to the south coast. Living in Camden had been brilliant and exciting (and very handy for Soho) for as long as I had been single or part of a carefree couple. But when you have the responsibility for a little life, your dog's or your baby's, you get concerned at the level of crime and drugs in the area. Dog theft was rife. We lived close to a needle exchange and often found syringes and drug paraphernalia on our basement stairs. We had a couple of local homeless guys who tried to sleep down there and even found the odd human poo now and again – I don't mind picking up Basil's but I draw the line at some old bloke's.

One scary night we had our front windows smashed by some kids running by, this scared Basil stupid and woke Stanley up screaming. We knew it was time to get them out of the Capital.

We said goodbye by presenting our regular London dog-walker with a picture of Basil in a silver photo frame from Tiffany (I hope she's replaced it with a picture of her children by now). She seemed quite sad to see Basil go, and we felt quite sad to be leaving. London had been my home for over 15 years and I had really felt part of that vibrant city.

But our new home by the seaside has delighted us all and we are incredibly lucky and happy to have found it. We have good friends in the area and my family are originally from there so it makes sense to us. My concerns at being close to the centre of town, bars, shops and friends has been replaced with the concern about proximity to outside spaces, the seafront and family friendly restaurants. We also have that most sought after of holiday destinations for many dog-owners a mere step from our front door, the Dog Beach! Yes, a seafront stretch that welcomes sun-seeking hounds all year long, which means we're able to paddle, picnic, sunbathe and swim with Basil whenever we like.

Brilliantly, the pubs outside of London seem a lot happier to allow dogs in and Basil is rarely turned away. We now have so many locals that on a walk Basil is running in and out of nearly every hostelry we pass. Yes, it's still embarrassing but always raises a smile and usually a comment from a passer-by such as '*He knows where he's going doesn't he?*'

Basil is a lot happier being close to such amazing walking spots like the beach and the South Downs. He has become part of a wonderful new dog walking family and has almost constant companionship with loving humans and friendly dogs, so I don't feel guilty about being at work in the day.

He doesn't come to the office with me anymore but that's only because I know in reality he's happier racing along the South Downs rather than sitting with a bone under my desk. Our new members of staff can't believe I used to bring a dog into the office every day and we often tell them stories about our 'Soho life'.

We now have a much more suitable family car complete with child seat, a big American diesel with a hatchback area for Basil to sit in. I can't believe we used to drive everywhere with him perched on my lap in the Porsche. But I will always have happy memories of him sitting next to me in the convertible, when it was just the two of us, the sun shining, music loud, the top down and us flying along, causing a stir. I wonder if he misses those days too?

Owning a dog changed my life. He completely slowed me down during a mad period in my life, probably just at the time I needed to rein myself in a bit. I was selfish, partying too hard and wildly ambitious. By falling in love with Basil I found my mind and heart opened up to other ambitions and all sorts of love I hadn't previously considered, so concerned was I with myself and my lifestyle. A small, growing feeling for something so wholly dependent on you and who loves you unconditionally really opened my eyes to the possibility of having a husband and a family. My dog was teaching me about life and I didn't even know it.

It seems that while I was obsessed with trying to fit a dog, husband and baby into my life without having to change my lifestyle so much, I really should have been considering what I could offer them. They give me so much in return. Being a party girl isn't that important to me now. I know I am thankful for the fun life I have led, I am sure I wouldn't be so happy with my calmer choices now had I not been quite so hedonistic in the past. I really miss my little single girl's Camden flat sometimes. I yearn for silence, the ability to do whatever I like and maybe a lie-in. But if I still lived there now the only company I might have would be an increasingly dwindling succession of gentleman callers and an ageing chinchilla.

Don't get me wrong I am not going *'gentle into that good night'*. I haven't hung my high heels up quite yet (although I can't wear them as often as I'd like because my feet have splayed out so much after carrying that enormous baby around for 9 months). I might not be able to afford the designer handbags anymore but I am back at work, albeit part time so I still get to spend days with Stanley and hang out in soft play areas. But it means I get to have time with my peers, go to the gym, drink coffee and be creative. And just as importantly talk about last night's television with my colleagues.

Happily, my very understanding business partner and I have been able to move our office to Brighton which means I am still close to Stanley and Basil in the day, even if I'm not thinking about them all of the time.

I've taken on a freelance writing job which I love and I'm in touch with my previous friends and contacts as much as ever before. Although everyone I used to hang around with are all pretty much married off now too, so we all expect less from each other and know how much harder it is to meet up. We still go on long boozy lunches in Soho now and again, but someone usually has a breastfeeding tot on their lap and I have to leave early to get back for nursery pick-up, but no one minds.

I've made some great new friends in Brighton who I go out drinking with regularly and I have even been to a few lovely star studded events where I've caught up with other industry pals and ended up in private member's bars laughing and singing until it was time to get the last train home. But now it's rarer and I'm not out every night I appreciate it a lot more.

I have to plan a watertight diary and get a lot of support from Patrick, work colleagues and babysitters as I balance work, nursery, my marriage and a social life. The social life comes last now but I make the most of it when I can.

I can feel a wry smile forming on my face as I make my way home from a day or night out much earlier than I would have done five years previously. I see the twenty-somethings getting ready for another event, jumping in a cab in all of their finery (and carrying new handbags no doubt), heading for the latest late night drinking spot that I know I won't have heard of. Time and places move on, and so do we all.

It might be only midnight but I know I am quite happy to go home (Basil is still waiting at the bottom of the stairs for me, no matter what time I come in, usually with one of Stanley's toys or the ubiquitous sock in his mouth). I find I need a lot more sleep now my days are taken up with all this home management and spending time at art classes with Stanley. Besides, hangovers at 40 are not what they were at the age of 20, or even 30. They are harder to get over the older you are (same with colds). Combine a hangover with a toddler and a dog bouncing on you and it's almost unbearable: an exquisite type of torture that those without children will not understand. I find I am almost unable to build Lego castles in the morning if I've had a night out. And if you know from first-hand experience what I am talking about then I am sorry for you too.

Patrick and I still enjoy a drink but we are now connoisseurs of drinking at home, a familiar habit of most parents I believe? And we even have babysitters now so we can still enjoy the odd 'date night', even if it's not every Saturday like it used to be. Besides a sad side-effect of pregnancy has left me unable to consume half as much alcohol as I used to. The woman who could easily drink from lunchtime through until 4am (and still book everyone a taxi) has been replaced by one who has to call time after one bottle of wine. I haven't been sick in the morning for years, and certainly not in my hat or my handbag!

A positive outcome of having a baby for Basil has been his parents are at home a lot more. As soon as Stanley is in bed he hops up onto the sofa for some 'tiddlywinks' knowing that in the evening he'll be as cosseted and cuddled as much as he ever was. He will still not be dissuaded from having his cuddle as he pushes himself up into our arms whether we like it or not. If Patrick and I are sitting on a two-seater sofa Basil will invariably wedge himself between us.

We now try to make as much of 'Basil time' as we can to ensure he always feels part of the family. Patrick is very keen that the dog is never left out of family outings or visits to friends, no matter how exasperating I sometimes find it having to accommodate a dog as well as a toddler (I hated having to keep poobags and a tripe stick in the plush new baby changing bag alongside the spare nappies and clean muslins).

As we all grow older and get a bit more set in our ways I'll admit I do find Basil rather irritating, especially when he manages to get his head in exactly the right position to stop the remote control working the TV. He can be a bit stupid and soppy sometimes and owning him causes us all a bit more work and concern than we would like. And he is always in the way, he doesn't move around as fast as he used to and because he is desperate not to be left out of any activity he always seems to be right under your feet. He can tell when we are getting ready to leave the house and will stand at the front door just to ensure we don't forget to take him along. For me sometimes it's a very fine line between *Good Boy* and *Bad Dog*!

We live very close to a large charity dog-re-homing centre in Shoreham and often the cry goes up in the house from me: *"You'll go to Shoreham if you're not careful"* and if we ever drive past it I make a big show of pretending to turn off in order to drop Basil off. Patrick always shouts in response *"Put your paws over your ears Basil"*. Obviously it would never happen (but don't tell him that).

Basil and Stanley have become great friends. Our son was always interested in the hairy creature that lived in our house and before he could even move he followed him with his eyes. Soon he was toddling about and trying to clutch at ears and chops and the little thumb-tail. Basil stoically ignored this invasion of his space apart from a rare snap or yelp to say the grabbing had gone too far. We've always leapt in to protect the dog more than Stanley. We know Basil would never harm a member of his much beloved pack, no matter how far beneath him he thinks the members are.

While we're at the vets a pained Basil would growl at the man in scrubs approaching him with a muzzle and he'll always try to see off the postman (such a cliché), but we who live in his home can touch him anywhere with impunity. I put my hands in his mouth to make sure he takes his tablets and I always kiss his face, I'm more likely to be bitten by a dinosaur than my dog.

Stanley's first discernible word that had a meaning was 'bar-bar' as he tried to frame the word 'Basil' while pointing at the dog. Soon every four legged creature we encountered on the street was called a 'bar-bar' and they were for a couple of years. Basil however is now 'Basil' and Stanley happily walks around the house yelling *'Get in Basil'*, *'Shut Up Basil'* and *'Move Basil'* in a telling display that lets Patrick know just how annoying I have found the dog that day!

Apart from the odd cursory sniff Basil tried to ignore our son for probably the first six months of his life. But slowly and surely he began to realise that the baby wasn't temporary and he accepted him into the household. He began to walk closely to the pushchair, standing in front of it when we stopped and became watchful of the soon toddling boy and would wait for him to catch up on a walk. I often catch the dog coming out of Stanley's room in the middle of the night as he goes on his rounds to check his family are ok.

Now the pair of them run around together, cuddle and are often both covered in glitter and paint. And there is even the hope that soon Stanley will be kicking a ball for Basil. I know he will achieve god-like status in the dogs' eyes the day that he does.

WHO WALKS WHO?

As Basil reaches his tenth birthday it's clear he is not the young pup he used to be, instead of running to the front door with a warning bark every time someone walks past he now makes do with an indignant huff from the comfort of the sofa just to let the neighbours know he's still got his eye on them. He's replaced reaction with a kind of bored nosiness as he sits on the bed in the day looking out of the window, in fact he's become an archetypal curtain twitcher in his old age.

Thankfully he has steered clear of any major illness or injury but there are a lot of grey hairs now around the muzzle and bad arthritis in one leg (Stanley says that it looks like Basil is 'hopping' when his painful limb hangs in the air). It sadly means that he can't get in and out of his dog flap as easily any more, but we don't mind the morning poo presents as much as we used to, we know it means he was in too much pain to hop in and out of the flap in the night. We still listen out of the clatter of the flap but not just to know he has used it but to make sure we hear him get back in because he can get trapped outside now. Unable to get back in the house he'll yip a bit to let us know when he needs some help (which is a bit annoying if you're in the bath or in bed). So we've made him another little step for the flap – like the one we made for him when he was a puppy – but this isn't because he can't reach the opening but because he needs a launch pad for his old bones!

But he still tries to act like youngster. He takes a bit longer to get going in the morning now but he still acts the clown. He still has a 'funny five minutes' when he zooms around the house madly for no reason. He can still bounce up and down like he is on springs. He still lies on his back with his limbs splayed inviting a rub or a kiss. He still sleeps on the bloody bed (but we have to lift him up onto it every night now because he finds it hard). He's still my boy.

We have discussed what will probably happen in a few years' time, Boxers don't usually live as long as other breeds. We're both a bit in denial, but we know the day that our merry foursome becomes a threesome is on the horizon.

By then it won't just be Patrick and I devastated, but Stanley too. He'll be old enough to have also fallen in love with the dog. It will be a difficult time for our young boy and we'll have to help him learn about love and loss. But in the tradition of Basil it means he'll still be teaching life lessons to those closest to him, right up until the end.

EPILOGUE: THE BEAUTY OF BASIL

My dog is beautiful to me, loving, sensitive and full of personality. He loves me and he loves his family. He has been there at some of our happiest and proudest moments, he has witnessed me at my worst and seen some things I wish he hadn't. But that simple love has never wavered.

He is responsible for the fact I spontaneously smile at every other dog I see in the street, affording me moments of involuntary joy every day.

He lives in our home, an autonomous, unknown, alien creature and yet a slave to our whims and the routine of our household. Always there, always in the background, never making a decision but the sole reason for so many decisions that are made.

He went from being the centre of our world, to an influence on the side-line. We went from taking hundreds of photos of Basil to thousands of photos of Stanley. But in nearly every one of those new pictures of our child you will see a white paw in the corner or a half a dog getting in the way as Basil, even if not centre stage, is still at the heart of the action.

As Stanley grows up to become more independent he will soon start pushing me away when I want a hug or a kiss. I can see him now as a surly eight year old muttering *'oh get off me mum'*. But I know Basil will always be up for a cuddle, he'll never push me away, he only ever wants to get closer.

As our human baby grows further from us into childhood, school and independence maybe I need to realise that our first 'baby' will always still be just that. Our baby. Well he still acts like a puppy for sure.

Come here boy... There's a good dog.

(see, I told you he didn't die)

NOT THE END

A BIG, BIG LOVE

ACKNOWLEDGEMENTS

I started writing this book many, many years ago. My family and I have been through a lot of changes during that time, so many that I constantly had to revise the words as we continued our journey through life. But the story will probably never really be told as our dog and child continue to grow and surprise us every day.

Maybe it could have been the book I continued to write forever, but I'm glad it is finally here for you to read. Thank you so much for taking the time. And besides, I really didn't want to be writing anything that made anyone (least of all me) cry in the bathroom...

More thanks go to a great friend and editor Dan Wilson, who made many welcome improvements, cut the flab and taught me about apostrophes. I claim all mistakes for my own.

Thank you to a wonderful Brighton artist and good friend Patrick O'Donnell (not my husband), who drew Basil so beautifully for the cover. You can always come dine with me.

Photographer extraordinaire Julia Claxton pulled everything together and created a fabulous front cover.

I know Basil would like to extend the paw of thanks to Lucy Reilly and Angela Hire for all the help, love and walks, as would I. You're part of the family!

Besides Patrick the other man in my life has to be my extraordinarily understanding business partner: Darren Whittaker. Our Company has been going longer than my marriage and I give thanks that he agreed to bringing a dog into our already mad world.

Before I had a dog I had friends, three of the best in fact. So I want to hail my life-long companions (who you will find in the pages of this book even if they are not named): Kate Duce, Kate Blagden and Tony Hannan.

Of course, I want to give all my love and thanks to the two humans I share my home with: Patrick and Stanley. Thank you for choosing me, I wish I deserved you.

And finally a big THANK YOU to all of the beautiful dogs out there, you all make the world a better place. But I'll save the biggest of all for the one who makes *my* world a better place, the one and only Basil.

You're better than a chinchilla.

Alice Wright, 2012

THANKS FOR READING OUR STORY!

For updates and more photos of Basil have a look at our Facebook page:

facebook.com/handbagsandpoobags

Update July 2018

But of course time marches on and takes those we love with it. Basil passed away on Tuesday the 3rd of October 2017 at 1.30pm.

He was 12 and a half, a long life for a Boxer apparently. And he managed to pack quite a lot of life into the five years since this book was first published, his story most definitely continued past the last page. As he grew older we booked family holidays in the UK so that he could come with us, he visited Cornwall, Dorset and even spent some time camping on an alpaca farm. He never did learn to swim but still wouldn't be left out of any activity.

He acquired a little brother, a white English Bulldog called Robert. The two never became great friends but managed to reach an understanding. Basil was in charge, he looked after the house and family and Robert was just the new fluffy baby. We're sure that keeping an eye on Robert was one of Basil's last duties and probably kept him alive a little longer.

We knew he wouldn't live forever; it was just that we couldn't ever imagine him not actually being around. Yes he'd slowed down a bit as he got older, got a little grumpier and illness began to cast its shadow. But we didn't mind taking him to the vet every week as his problems mounted. Even with a grey face and slower pace he was still Basil. He still loved us and we him. He was still always up for a cuddle. He still wouldn't eat or sleep until everyone was home. He still loved to run and play ball.

And then the day came when he collapsed whilst playing with that beloved football. As he was already on heart medication we knew it was time to put the ball away for good. And then he couldn't make it down the stairs to go to the toilet in time. And then he couldn't get off the sofa as his feet curled in on themselves. And then he was barely eating. And then we knew it was time. Were we only keeping him alive because we didn't want him to die? And so I booked an appointment.

Friends who knew Basil visited the night before and we took pictures, he managed a little bit of crispy duck (his favourite!) but it felt unreal. And on the chosen day I didn't believe for one minute that he would actually die, that he would actually leave us. Stanley kissed him goodbye before school and as we took a final walk, just Patrick, Basil and I, no phones, no one else, we drank tea in the autumn sun and innocent as to our intentions Basil trod his usual route as if it was any other day. Even the nurse said it didn't have to be the end if there was another way. Of course there would be another way. But the vet said we were only heading one way. He had slowed down enough now to stop, we had to let him go.

I wrote about what happened on that day, something to mark the occasion and what I was feeling. I was as honest as I could be about that painful 24 hours. As a blogger for Metro it was published online there and I include it at the end of this chapter because it describes the immediate passing of Basil better than I can again here nearly a year later.

The response we had from friends who knew him and comments from those who didn't was extraordinary (including this book's lovely Facebook group). If you've lost your own beloved pet you recognise the same pain in others. No one suggested that he was 'just a dog' because I am not sure sharing a home with a living and loving creature for over 12 years means they are 'just' an anything. He was so much more than just a dog, he changed our lives.

The days after were difficult for all of us. I was surprised by the wave of feeling that tugged at the family. In fact it was amazing to feel such grief, to be reminded that you can feel something so strongly, to know that those emotional muscles still work when you haven't had to flex them for a long time.

There was a big black space on the sofa that I couldn't look at. A big black space by the side of the bed where he slept. And yes, a big black space in the family. I began to worry about what would happen to us all, Basil ran the household, he looked out for us, he kept us safe and everything just felt normal when he was around. I had genuine panics that we wouldn't cope without him. But we have managed day by day, crying and laughing.

The day I picked Basil's ashes up from the vets was bittersweet. The kind nurses who had held me whilst I cried showed me the bruises I had left on their arms so tight had I gripped them. But they said it had been an honour. I gave them biscuits and they gave me a huge heavy box which I carried home in my arms. It began to rain and I began to cry. It felt like the longest walk as the box got heavier and wetter. Inside was actually just lots of very heavy brochures and one tiny tin of ashes which I could have just held in my hand. Such a little tin to hold such a big life.

We did say we would scatter him in a park, or across the lawns he loved so much opposite our house. However, we aren't ready to let him go yet and he sits in the front room to still keep an eye on us all. And of course we have pictures of him everywhere, his collar is still hanging up and his Christmas decoration packed away ready to be rediscovered every year.

Now we can talk about him without crying, we just miss him. Sometimes when alone I just say his name out loud. Patrick is adamant we will own another Boxer. Stanley now nearly a teenager hasn't lived a day without a dog in his life and Basil set a good standard for him. Robert hasn't taken well to position of top dog in the house and has become suspicious and grumpy since Basil died, but trained as he was by the master now shows some of his traits: he feels the same about food, the neighbours and family herding as Basil did. We like to think that we'll be able to identify a bit of Basil in every dog we have in the future as Robert passes on what he knows.

Walks are still difficult as we pass Basil's favourite spots or we're suddenly hit by a memory. Seeing another Boxer dog makes our heads turn and our tummies flip. My hand still automatically reaches into the space between Patrick and I where Basil's head would always be, now it's empty. When other dog walkers approach to talk about Robert I want to tell them that we had another dog, that we had a Boxer too called Basil. Remember at the beginning of the book how I hated to accosted by those who had lost dogs? With Basil still a puppy I didn't want to be touched by their pain. Now I am that person, with that pain.

But I understand it now, the life you live with a dog can change you, you want to talk about it. What a privilege it gives you, to share the life of an animal in its entirety? You will never experience your children growing from babies to become older than you, but with Basil we shared his whole existence. His life and his death our responsibility.

And so now we are at the end of his story, which I have hidden here at the very end of the book hoping that you wouldn't find it, that you would have the same experience past readers have had, never reaching the end. I promised the dog wouldn't die at the beginning of the book and I didn't lie because the real story was Basil's life, and ours with him. I hope you still enjoyed it?

I've been dreading writing this - the final chapter - for the past ten months because that last full stop will be the end of our journey together. However, its not the end of the journey for us as dog owners, Robert is nearly four now and we have a new puppy! Douglas the Pug, a charming little chap who has cheered us all, was born within hours of Basil dying (not that we knew it at the time) and while he'll never know him maybe will benefit from all that we learnt from owning that old Boxer dog. Yes we made a lot of mistakes but we got by.

However, it seems we're still ignoring all good advice about dogs and making our own rash decisions... Douglas was bought as a Christmas present for Stanley. And what does the famous line remind us? 'A Dog is For Life, Not Just For Christmas'. Well thinking about it I am sure they mean the dog's life, not ours, because there isn't a dog alive who could live long enough for those who love it.

Goodnight boy, you were a very very good dog indeed.

Published on Metro.co.uk, Wednesday 4 Oct 2017 2:24 pm
My dog died today – did I love him enough? And who will take care of us now? By Alice Wright

My dog died today. I knew he was going to, I'd booked the appointment the day before. You get given the last appointment, the 'death slot', so as the vet waiting room empties out only you and your dog are left. No one else to witness your loss.

I got dressed up, put on some make-up, some perfume. I don't know why but it seemed appropriate to have made an effort. But of course he didn't know or care what I wore, just that I was there.

His name was Basil, he was a big bouncing boxer dog. He liked footballs, chicken and to sleep on our bed. He'd been failing for a while, slowing down, losing weight, heart troubles, neurological damage. But he'd hung on in there, every time we thought it was over he'd surprised us, another new drug, another new day. He'd rallied so often we joked that in the past year he'd had more renaissances than a French king.

He was stubborn. I knew he didn't want to die, he didn't want to leave us. The latest sudden downturn made us realise he wasn't infallible. Maybe he wouldn't always be around, maybe it wasn't fair letting him keep hanging on. And so, yes, I booked the appointment because if you love your dog that's what you do, right? But as we clipped on his lead for that last time he seemed happy for another excursion, stronger, interested and excited. Trusting. He enjoyed the walk, the sun on his face, took a roll in the grass. 'Look,' I said, 'there's still walks to be had, chicken to be eaten. He's rallied again. The King rises.' It was inconceivable we'd walk out of the vets again without him. Surely?

I thought of the occasions I had booked long overdue hairdresser appointments only to wake up that day with fabulous dreamy hair. Damn!

'Typical,' said the vet. Yes, typical.

'But you still get your hair cut though, don't you?' suggested my husband.

'We're only heading in one direction,' said the vet.

And so if not now, when? Now while he was still happy, still enjoying the sun? Or the bitter, bitter end? A snapped leg, a cardiac event, a collapse in his own mess?

'Of course not,' I said. And so it was today.

My husband held him in a bear hug, while I looked into his eyes and thanked him, told him how proud I was of him, that I loved him. I love you Basil. Still trusting he didn't struggle, he looked back into my eyes until his eyes didn't see me any more. The next half an hour is a blur. I didn't want to see his body. That warm, sweet-smelling fur that no longer held our Basil.

Thank goodness there was no one else to witness our loss because there weren't enough tears in the world at that moment.

'A good death,' said the vet. A good life, I hoped.

After sharing a home with him for over 12 years it feels unbelievable he won't be on the sofa or in his bed now. So familiar he was almost invisible, part of every day and every celebration, but his steady presence made our home what it was. We trusted him. He looked after us, he wouldn't go to bed until we were all tucked up, he wouldn't eat until we were all home, he warned us of strangers outside. He was the chosen night-time companion for insomnia, the go-to for a cuddle. A buffer for all arguments. He loved us utterly and completely.

While I grew frustrated with his ageing, his slowness, his mess, he would still limp into the kitchen to thank me for dinner, would still valiantly bark at would-be intruders, would still drag himself up and down the stairs to welcome us home or put us to bed. He was still being Basil.

And yet we'd airily discuss all the things we could do when Basil had gone, knowing that of course he would at some point be gone. Maybe a new carpet. A foreign holiday possibly? But those stupid, ignorant discussions didn't take into account the reality of Basil actually being gone. And now he is I would give any new carpet or foreign holiday for him to still be here.

Did he know that? Did I love him enough while he was still here? He looked after us, but did I look after him? And who is going to take care of us all now?

I am broken, in physical pain. My husband is inconsolable in the kitchen at the loss of his best friend. Our nine-year-old child – whose first word was an approximation of Basil and who has never lived a day without him – seemed to shrug off the news to reach for the iPad to look at some possible new puppies. I've just found that same child crying strongly in their bedroom. The bedroom Basil used to check on his nightly rounds. But not anymore.

My dog died today. But it wasn't just my dog that died today.

THE END

Printed in Great Britain
by Amazon